At Issue

Does the U.S. Two-Party System Still Work?

Other Books in the At Issue Series:

At Issue

Does the U.S. Two-Party System Still Work?

Noah Berlatsky, Book Editor

GREENHAVEN PRESS
A part of Gale, Cengage Learning

GALE
CENGAGE Learning™

Detroit • New York • San Francisco • New Haven, Conn • Waterville, Maine • London

GALE
CENGAGE Learning™

Christine Nasso, *Publisher*
Elizabeth Des Chenes, *Managing Editor*

© 2010 Greenhaven Press, a part of Gale, Cengage Learning.

Gale and Greenhaven Press are registered trademarks used herein under license.

For more information, contact:
Greenhaven Press
27500 Drake Rd.
Farmington Hills, MI 48331-3535
Or you can visit our Internet site at gale.cengage.com

For product information and technology assistance, contact us at

Gale Customer Support, 1-800-877-4253
For permission to use material from this text or product, submit all requests online at
www.cengage.com/permissions

Further permissions questions can be emailed to permissionrequest@cengage.com

Articles in Greenhaven Press anthologies are often edited for length to meet page requirements. In addition, original titles of these works are changed to clearly present the main thesis and to explicitly indicate the author's opinion. Every effort is made to ensure that Greenhaven Press accurately reflects the original intent of the authors. Every effort has been made to trace the owners of copyrighted material.

Cover photograph © Images.com/Corbis.

LIBRARY OF CONGRESS CATALOGING-IN-PUBLICATION DATA

Does the U.S. two-party system still work? / Noah Berlatsky, book editor.
    p. cm. -- (At issue)
    Includes bibliographical references and index.
    ISBN 978-0-7377-4644-0 (hardcover) -- ISBN 978-0-7377-4645-7 (pbk.)
    1. Political parties--United States. 2. Two party systems--United States. I. Berlatsky, Noah.
    JK2265.D64 2010
    324.273--dc22
                                            2009038623

Printed in the United States of America
1 2 3 4 5 6 7 13 12 11 10 09

Contents

Introduction

In considering the answer to the question, "Does the U.S. two-party system still work?" one must first answer another: What does it mean to say that government "works"? To say the government works can refer to its ability to function effectively. From this perspective, a working government is one that can pass legislation reflecting the will of the majority, that can provide essential services to its citizens, and that can respond swiftly and decisively to domestic and international crises.

Some commentators argue that the U.S. two-party system—presently composed of the Republican and Democratic political parties—does not work because ingrained partisan differences prevent the performance of fundamental governmental duties. For instance, Herbert G. Klein, former editor-in-chief of Copley Newspapers, writes in a 2006 article for the American Enterprise Institute for Public Policy Research Web site (www.aei.org), "Extreme partisanship endangers the function of all three branches of federal government—the presidency, the Congress and even the courts. Confirmation is blocked on a regular basis on federal judgeships and even the Supreme Court."

But other writers contend that the U.S. government does work effectively. They point out, for example, that voters do not vote directly for a president in U.S. presidential elections; rather, the election depends on a state-level system of elected and appointed officials who vote for whichever presidential candidate wins the popular election in a given state. This institution is known as the Electoral College, and it is an important aspect of the political system in the United States. Writing in the *Wall Street Journal* in 2008, David Lewis Schaefer maintains that the Electoral College "contributes to effective presidential leadership and representative government."

Other commentators consider the issue of whether or not government "works" in terms of fairness and justice. For this group, functionality depends on how well the government represents its citizens, whether it treats everyone equally and protects them from discrimination, and how susceptible government is to corruption. In this regard, some view the U.S. two-party system as a principal enabler of inequality and corruption. In a 2008 speech (reported by Seema Mehta in the *Los Angeles Times*), independent presidential candidate Ralph Nader derided Republicans and Democrats as a "two-party dictatorship" and demanded, "How many more decades are we going to give them before we get rid of this least-worst, this lesser-of-two-evils mind set and start breaking this corporate grip . . . and have alternative candidates from alternative parties that stand as if people mattered first and foremost?"

Despite the vehement criticism of third-party advocates such as Nader, not everyone considers the current U.S. political system a failure. Indeed, some observers believe the two-party system helps to ensure political fairness and decency. For example, in the 2002 collection *Multiparty Politics in America: Prospects and Performance*, John F. Bibby wrote an essay titled "In Defense of the Two-Party System." In this piece, Bibby argues that, "Because candidate recruitment and political advancement in the United States are primarily through the two major parties, the likelihood of demagogues and extremist candidates either winning major-party nominations or being elected is reduced."

It is important to note that these two aspects of the two-party system—whether it's effective and just—do not necessarily have to be mutually exclusive. In fact, when evaluating the merits and demerits of the current political system, commentators often make arguments that rely on both governmental effectiveness and fairness. When Bibby compliments the two-party system, he does so in terms of demonstrating how partisanship can be fair and effective. He writes, "Policy making . . . requires extensive negotiation, bargaining, compromise, and cross-party alliances. . . . It is hard to imagine how introducing a substantial number of third- or fourth-party representatives into the mix would facilitate more timely and effective policy making."

Opponents of the two-party system also combine elements of fairness and effectiveness in their critiques of the current political establishment. In an essay published on the Web site Intellectual Conservative (www.intellectualconservative.com) and titled "The Two-Party System: A Catastrophic Failure," Justin Soutar argues that "The Republican and Democratic parties have divided the American people over fundamental moral values, they have failed to rectify longstanding national problems, and their existence chiefly benefits special interest groups, politicians, and mega-corporate executives." In Soutar's judgment, the two-party system does not work because it is both ineffective and corrupt.

Other critical opinions range from a resigned acceptance of the status quo to indignation at the injustice of the two-party system. Writing in *Newsweek* in February 2009, Yuval Levin argues that, while partisanship is not always effective, it is essential to democracy. Further, he admits, "At its best, the partisan fray expresses the maturity of our political life; and even at its worst (which is to say, most of the time) it is a better way to govern ourselves than the pursuit at all costs of an elusive technocratic consensus." By contrast, Shamus Cooke, in an article published on the Peace, Earth & Justice News Web site (www.pej.org) in December 2007, declares that "The key fact that helps explain the policies of the Democrats is that they, like the Republicans, are parties that represent the capitalist class." For Cooke, who writes from a socialist perspective, both parties function effectively only for the elite class, and in doing so they perpetuate injustice against the working class.

When political commentators evaluate the U.S. two-party system, they not only express an opinion about the present state of American government, but they also convey a pointed ideological position on the role and purpose of government as a whole. Whereas some writers emphasize pragmatic effectiveness, others underscore the importance of moral justice and equality, and still others try to balance these concerns in various ways. A discussion of the effectiveness of the U.S. two-party system, then, is a discussion not only about one mode of government, but about broader philosophies, ideals, and hopes associated with American democracy.

1

Polarized Parties Are Good for America

Matthew Yglesias

Matthew Yglesias is a liberal blogger and writer specializing in American politics and public policy. His work has appeared in numerous publications, including The Atlantic Monthly, The American Prospect, *and the* New York Times. *His blog currently is hosted by the Center for American Progress, and he is the author of* Heads in the Sand: How the Republicans Screw Up Foreign Policy and Foreign Policy Screws Up the Democrats.

Strong coherent political parties are beneficial because they make it easier for voters to predict the outcome of their votes. In the 1950s, when party views were arguably less clear, voters had more difficulty making their preferences known, especially on issues of race and racism, about which the parties were internally divided. It is not voters, but party elites who benefit from weak parties. When parties are weak, influential individuals can build coalitions that enhance their own influence and prestige.

In 1950, the American Political Science Association's Committee on Political Parties issued a clarion call, "Toward a More Responsible Two-Party System," that today sounds quaint. The committee worried about insufficient party discipline and undue tolerance of dissent from the party line, arguing that the country needed political parties with "sufficient internal cohesion" to carry out their legislative agendas. The report urged the minority party to draw starker policy contrasts with the majority, and to act "as the critic of the party in power."

In short, the political scientists of the time wanted polarization. They got it, of course, and the result, in the general view, has been unseemly and unwelcome. Polarized politics takes the form of a bitter, endless feud; cross-party alliances, once the mainstay of Washington life, are now rare. Yet as today's presidential candidates call for a less divisive kind of politics, it's worth recalling the 1950s. While polarization has its drawbacks, the alternative is often worse.

The Past Was Not Less Contentious, Just Less Coherent

The mid-20th century is sometimes remembered as an era of cozy political consensus, but in fact the corridors of power echoed then with starkly disparate voices. Some officials advocated central planning of the economy in all but name; others wanted no federal safety net whatsoever. And of course, the country's elected representatives were as deeply divided over civil rights as their constituents were. The politics were no less contentious than they are today. They were just less coherent.

The looser partisanship of the period was mostly the result of racism and its complex role in the politics of the time. The legacy of the Civil War had made the Democrats the party of southern white supremacists, but the legacy of the New Deal had also made them the party of northern liberals and many urban African Americans. These latter constituencies were demanding federal intervention in southern affairs to secure the rights of southern blacks. At the same time, many members of the GOP [Republican party]—the traditional home of black voters and the party of racial progress in many states—were resisting these demands, which struck them as violating the principle of a modest federal government.

The result was a muddle. Nearly every congressional representative from the South was a Democrat and an opponent of civil rights, irrespective of his or her views about anything else. So while most Democrats were to the left of Republicans on economic and foreign-policy issues, many were more conservative than the average Republican on matters of race. Racial liberals and racial conservatives could be found in both parties.

Polarization Is Bad for Elites

Since the 1970s, however, the significance of civil-rights conflicts in American elections has declined sharply. As older representatives left Congress in the 1980s, political divisions became cleaner. Ideologically moderate politicians have not disappeared, but relatively conservative Democrats like Senators Ben Nelson [NE] and Mary Landrieu [LA] are, on most issues, now to the left of relatively liberal Republicans such as Susan Collins [ME] and Olympia Snowe [ME]. The meet-in-the-middle overlap is gone.

In a polarized world, elections and procedural rules largely determine policy outcomes; there's little room for self-styled players to construct coalitions on the fly, and enhance their own power in the process.

From a journalistic point of view, the resulting system is tragically dull. Legislative outcomes become a simple matter of vote-counting: either a party has a majority or it doesn't. There's little room for journalistic sleuthing, and what stories there are to tell lack the color and drama of, say, *Charlie Wilson's War* [a 2007 film based on a true story] in which an extremely hawkish Democratic congressman was able to persuade his party's leadership to back a massive covert war in Afghanistan.

For veteran Washington hands—wheelers and dealers in the lobbying game or at the major interest groups—the new system is worse than dull. It's emasculating. This is why political elites find polarization so distasteful. In a polarized world, elections and procedural rules largely determine policy outcomes; there's little room for self-styled players to construct coalitions on the fly, and enhance their own power in the process. The growth in the lobbying industry might seem to belie the point, but consider Tom DeLay's post-1994 "K Street Project"—which pressured lobbying firms who wanted access on the Hill to hire more Republicans—or the swing of the pendulum back after the Democratic takeover in 2006. Power in Congress is firmly in the hands of the party leadership; lobbyists become less powerful, not more, in a polarized system.

Polarization Is Good for Voters

But for voters, the boring new ways can be looked at in another way—they're straightforward. Elections have a predictable and easy-to-understand relationship to government action. Electing a Democrat means, on the margin, more spending on the federal safety net and more government regulation, while electing a Republican produces policies more favorable to business interests. You don't necessarily get everything you want (ask any liberal disappointed by the continued flow of funds for the Iraq War), but at least on domestic measures, things move predictably.

Most democracies have at least three parties represented in their legislatures. That gives people more choices, while still giving them coherent choices.

Under the looser system, it was hard to know where the parties really stood, or what effect elections might have. In 1956, for example, the voters of Idaho turned out their incumbent conservative Republican senator, Herman Welker, in favor of the Democrat Frank Church, whose liberal views included strong support for civil rights. Church's election helped preserve the Democratic Party's slender majority in the Senate, despite pickups by several Republicans. But as a result, the Judiciary Committee—with its jurisdiction over civil-rights issues—came under the gavel of Mississippi's James Eastland, a die-hard segregationist.

In the same election, both Dwight Eisenhower and Adlai Stevenson had obtained substantial support from African Americans *and* segregationists. Both parties were nominally supportive of civil rights, and yet little of consequence was accomplished in the ensuing years. What's more, it was unclear to voters what course of action might break this inertia. Party affiliation was important because the majority party won the chairmanships of powerful committees that controlled many levers of government. Inconveniently, however, party affiliation didn't align tightly with ideology, leaving much of the real business of the country to be decided behind closed doors in Washington.

The Problem Is Not Partisanship, But Too Few Parties

Of course, today's choice between two prix fixe ideological menus doesn't make everyone happy. Indeed, almost nobody agrees with either party's basic orientation on all questions facing the country. This breeds disgruntlement with the reductive nature of America's party system. But the real complaint here is not with the coherence of the parties, but with the quantity of them. Most democracies have at least three parties represented in their legislatures. That gives people more choices, while still giving them coherent choices.

That said, what usually causes the rise of new parties, or the loosening and confusion of existing ones, is the emergence of new social conflicts that are so overwhelmingly important that they strain the existing coalitions, scrambling party positions on everything else. Despite the ferocious rhetoric, the new issues of recent years—primarily related to sex and religion—haven't been controversial enough to disturb the existing alignment. Perhaps religion will one day do that, causing the depolarization of the parties along economic and foreign-policy lines, or the rise of a viable third party in some states. But of course, this cure for polarized parties would be worse than the disease. Strong clashes between coherent parties aren't a sign that the country is flying apart—they mean we're getting along better than we think.

2

The U.S. Electoral System Must Be Reformed to Make Third Parties Feasible

Jerry Fresia

Jerry Fresia is a painter and art instructor. Previously, he was a professor of political science. His book, Toward an American Revolution: Exposing the Constitution and Other Illusions, *was published in 1999.*

It is nearly impossible to elect third-party candidates because U.S. political institutions are designed in a way that discourages the existence of more than two political parties. To make third-party candidacies viable, the United States should abandon the Electoral College, single-member districts (in which the winner of the election is awarded all of the votes), and plurality elections (in which the person with the most votes, even if he or she does not secure a majority of votes, wins.) These changes would make third parties viable and also would make the United States more democratic.

Again and again progressives step forward to remind us of how bad the Democratic Party, or at least its leadership, is. The point of the lament is to encourage the support of third party candidates and parties.

This type of analysis is troubling, not because its analysis of the Democratic party is incorrect, but because the analysis leaves unexamined the institutional arrangement that makes a

Jerry Fresia, "Third Parties?" *Z Magazine*, February 28, 2006. Reproduced by permission of the author.

vibrant third party at the federal level impossible. Never in American history has a third party captured the presidency. The Republican success in 1860 was anomalous in that one of the two major parties was simply torn apart by the divisions that issued in the Civil War soon after.

The possible election of Bernie Sanders as an Independent senator from Vermont is also anomalous [Editor's note: Sanders was elected to the U.S. Senate in 2006.]. Vermont, in terms of population is essentially a congressional district. Sander's Independent Party is not a national or oppositional party. In fact, it may be in virtue of Sanders' distance from progressive third parties—the nominal independence from politics—that wins him broad support in a small state.

So here is my point: our political institutions were designed to give the appearance of public participation while preventing its substance. The two party system is part of that design. Encouraging third party participation makes sense only if it is one element in a campaign to establish democratic institutions in the US. With that in mind, let's take a look at the three central institutional features of our political system that ensure at the federal level that only two parties will ever have a real chance of governing. They are the Electoral College, single-member districts and plurality elections.

The Electoral College Makes Third Parties Impossible

On four occasions in US history, the candidate with the most popular votes did not win the presidency. This is a feature of a republican form of government, a government that is intended to "check" popular participation and "level" our democratic impulses. The mechanism by which this is done is the Electoral College. The Electoral College also ensures that the number of parties seriously competing for the presidency will always be and only be two.

Each State's allotment of electors is equal to the number of House members to which it is entitled plus two Senators (with the District of Columbia getting three). But here is the key element for our purposes: in order to win the presidency, a candidate must win a majority of electors.

By requiring that a candidate win a majority, the Electoral College guarantees that third parties must do one of three things. Let's assume a third party arises and is incredibly strong (the [Ross] Perot candidacy that for a time was pushing 20 percent nationally), but has no realistic chance of winning a majority of electors straight out. Its first choice is to press forward, win a significant percentage of electors and deny either of the two major parties a majority victory. In this case, the election would be decided by the House of Representatives, already dominated by the major parties. Option 1: third party loses everything.

The second option, again assuming a strong third party, is to coalesce with one of the major parties in order to get something. Arguably the most powerful progressive political party was the People's Party during the late 19th century. In 1896, they had anywhere from 25 to 45 percent strength in twenty-odd states. Clearly unable to win the presidency as a third party, they felt compelled to coalesce with the Democrats and saw their more radical labor and socialist elements purged in a losing effort. Well, there you are. Option 2 puts you back inside one of the major parties.

At the city level, proportional systems of representation have encouraged greater popular participation.

The third option arises when a third party is not that strong, say a [Ralph] Nader [Green Party] candidacy of 2000. We know what happens there. A weak third party, by taking votes away from the party closest to it ideologically will, in effect, help elect the major party most unlike themselves. Option 3: help the other guys win.

Single-Member Districts Cripple Third Parties

Single-member districts simply mean that in any given district, the winner takes all. That is, if the Republicans get 42 percent in a congressional district and the Democrats get 36 percent and the Greens get 22 percent, the district will still be represented by a single member, in this case the Republican. This is not terribly democratic as you can see. The majority of voters (Democrat and Green or 58 percent) garner zero representation. . . .

Single-member districts, of course, stand in contrast to proportional representation, which permits third parties to gain a foothold in proportion to their strength. Prior to 1842, we should note, single-member districts in the House of Representatives did not exist in Alabama, Georgia, Mississippi, Missouri, New Hampshire, New Jersey and Rhode Island. In these states, the entire congressional delegation was elected at large by means of what was called a general ticket. A return to the election of state delegations at large might lend itself nicely to proportional representation. In any case, we can see that the current arrangement is not carved in stone.

Majority elections have resulted in many progressive candidate and third party victories at the local level.

At the city level, proportional systems of representation have encouraged greater popular participation. In New York City from 1936 to 1947, proportional representation resulted in the participation of the American Labor Party, the Liberal Party, the Communist Party and the Fusion forces. In addition to a number of blacks, two Communists were elected to the city council. That did it. Business forces restored the two party system, the only true "democratic" form of party participation as they put it.

Plurality Elections Also Hurt Third Parties

Plurality elections mean that the candidate with the most votes wins. Unless the third party candidate is about to out poll the Democrat or Republican, supporters of third parties get no representation. Zero. Moreover, with this in mind, we are often told that voting our conscience is tantamount to throwing our vote away or electing "the other guy." For example, if [former presidents] George [W.] Bush, Bill Clinton and [American linguist and philosopher] Noam Chomsky were to run (and could) for governor of California, the odds are pretty good that Noam would come in third. And there would be a very intense debate over whether or not we should vote for Clinton or Noam. This is the curse of plurality elections.

So let's call the bastards on their professed support for democracy. Dump the Electoral College, push for proportional representation, and adopt majority elections.

However, there are numerous mayoral elections where "majority election" rules obtain. Majority elections (sometimes called the "double primary") require a second ballot if no candidate gets a majority in the first round. This scheme encourages third parties because you are encouraged to vote your conscience in the hope that your party might at least come in second, in which case there would be a second ballot or runoff between the top two vote getters. And if the progressive party didn't make it that far, then one could choose the lesser of two evils in the final round. Majority elections have resulted in many progressive candidate and third party victories at the local level.

21

Make Elections More Democratic

There are many different ways of organizing elections throughout the world. The electoral system in the United States has been shaped to both reduce popular participation and advance business interests. The impulse to create third party oppositional politics is natural, positive, and will persist until space for oppositional politics is created. However, to assume that our system is democratic and that the creation of oppositional politics turns only on a matter of will as opposed to a reform of our institutions is to advocate moral victory and political failure.

None of our rights have been handed down; they have all been won through resistance. So let's call the bastards on their professed support for democracy. Dump the Electoral College, push for proportional representation and adopt majority elections, already in practice around the country at the local level, for federal office. Third parties yes, but not without a corresponding demand for democratic elections here in the US of A.

3

Third-Party Campaigns Can Hurt Liberals and Everyday People

G. William Domhoff

G. William Domhoff is a research professor at the University of California, Santa Cruz. His 1965 book Who Rules America? *is a classic sociology text, and the fifth edition was released in 2006. Among his many other books are* The Power Elite and the State: How Policy Is Made in America *(1990) and* Changing the Powers That Be: How the Left Can Stop Losing and Win *(2003).*

Left-liberals and leftists need to project a strong egalitarian platform and vision in order to succeed as a Third-Party candidate. For example, Ralph Nader justified his presidential run in 2000 on the grounds that the Republicans and Democrats are not all that different and on the belief that a Democratic loss would punish Democratic leaders and push them further to the left. These positions are based on a moralistic refusal to accept the realities of electoral politics. Among those realities is the fact that Republican victories hurt the low-income people whom Nader claimed to be helping. By insisting on working outside the Democratic party, and by his moralistic rhetoric and actions, Nader damaged his own liberal cause.

G. William Domhoff, "Third Parties Don't Work: Why and How Egalitarians Should Transform the Democratic Party," *Who Rules America?* March 2005. Reproduced by permission.

Since the article was first written in March 2005, and is now being published in this book in 2010, readers have the opportunity to see where it fits with what has happened since 2005 and where it doesn't. I think it remains exactly right in claiming that activists have to transform the Democratic Party if they hope to bring more equality and social justice to the United States. In that sense, Barack Obama's historic victory in 2008 and the increasing number of liberal Democrats in Congress are a fulfillment of the vision projected in this article. However, the most vigorous activists have stayed outside the party and the left-liberals and leftists within it have not projected a strong egalitarian vision or figured out how to use the party more effectively. On those matters, the potential remains unfulfilled. The Democratic Party is at best a centrist party that leans slightly leftward on a few issues. The corporate rich still rule America.

Would a Third-Party Work in the United States?

Since the Democratic Party has now shed its Southern racist wing, and machine Democrats are mostly a thing of the past, it cannot be just historical memories that keep egalitarians from seeing the golden opportunity provided by party primaries. So something else must be going on as well. I think that the something else is based in the strong moral sense that characterizes most egalitarian activists. Indeed, a moral outrage over the issues highlighted in egalitarian social movements is the most important thing they all share in common. It is an essential source of their energy and courage in facing great danger, but it also can be a hindrance because they cannot tolerate much compromise on the issues of concern to them, especially if they think people have failed to stand up for their beliefs. As speeches, articles, and letters-to-the-editor by third-party advocates make abundantly clear, they see the

Democrats as compromised, corrupt, and spineless. In this sense, egalitarians are "purists," and usually proud of it.

This moral zeal creates a strong inclination to separate from the everyday world and create an alternative set of standards and institutions. It generates a desire for a distinctive social identity and a space to call one's own, such as a third party. In addition, strong moral outrage creates a sense of immediacy that reinforces the preference for a third party as a way to express exasperation with compromise. As a result, egalitarians often become very annoyed with the liberal politicians who share most of their values and programs. As egalitarians say again and again, they want to be able to vote their "conscience," not the "lesser of two evils." The tensions that therefore arise between egalitarians and liberals within the electoral arena then become a hindrance to a general movement for egalitarian social change.

Moral indignation contributes to a preference for a third party in still another way. When changes do not come quickly, the activists' sense of frustration grows, especially when many of the low-income and average-income who are most exploited are slow to join the movement. The thought then arises that it takes strong medicine to "wake people up," to make them "realize" how badly they are being treated. What often follows is the conclusion that something drastic is necessary to shake people up, like a depression or a conservative Republican administration, so they can summon the energy to act in what egalitarians are sure are the best interests of the mistreated or downtrodden people they are trying to help. In short, they end up with a new theory: "the worse things are, the better the chances for egalitarian social change." Call it "the-worse-the-better" theory.

The-worse-the-better theory combines with moral purism to create a preference for leftist third parties that supposedly will heighten the tensions by forcing people to face life under the harshest representatives of the capitalist class, the Republicans. In the context of a conflicted, cautious and declining Democratic Party, it is thought that people will turn to the new third party as they grow weary of Republican rule. Contrary to this belief, egalitarians in the United States have done far better when moderates are in charge of the government because there is a greater possibility that social movements can have a positive effect on the political system. This was first seen very dramatically during the New Deal, when union organizers were able to take advantage of mildly liberal labor legislation to create many new unions and pressure for the improved labor law that created the National Labor Relations Board in 1935. It is also shown by the fact that progressives did not prosper in the long winter of [Ronald] Reagan-[George H.W.] Bush rule from 1981 to 1993.

And if any further proof were needed, look at the disastrous situation in which everyone from the center to the far left found themselves with the second [George w.] Bush Administration in charge. This is the best evidence against the worse-the-better theory that could be imagined. But the past evidence against the theory, such as futile third-party presidential campaigns in 1948, 1968, and 1980, was soon forgotten, and there is always the danger that it will be forgotten again in the future unless left activists have a perspective that takes the structure of the electoral system seriously. Right now many of them still don't. Just take a look at the Green Party, still talking about moving beyond the local level. Or listen to Medea Benjamin and Kevin Danaher at Global Exchange in San Francisco, who remain strong advocates of a third party, building for the long run, as Danaher explained to me. (Note added in 2009: Some of these people have muted their calls for a third party because Barack Obama is an African-American, but you can be sure that there are still virtually no American leftists who have abandoned their belief in the need for a progressive third party.)

The moral outrage that leads in the direction of third parties is understandable and admirable in the face of huge inequalities and unnecessary suffering, but there are better ways to express it and at the same time be more effective in the political arena. The first need is to make a distinction between activists and liberal politicians, and to see that they have different but complementary roles in bringing about egalitarian social change. Second, it is necessary to create a distinctive social identity and organizational space within the Democratic Party, not outside it.

An Egalitarian Movement

Activists, to be effective, have to be uncompromising moralists who stand up for their principles. They are exemplars who break unjust laws when need be, and here of course the premier American examples are Martin Luther King, Jr., and other leaders of the early Civil Rights Movement. Although Ralph Nader in his days was a great consumer and environmentalist he did not break unjust laws and go to jail, saying he preferred "to be a plaintiff rather than a defendant," he was in fact a moral exemplar. He sacrificed his everyday life to the civic causes he worked on every hour of the day, using the money he made from books and speeches to build new organizations that have had a measurable impact on the day-to-day lives of millions of Americans. As an activist, he was heroic. As a politician, he was a destructive, head-strong fool.

From their stance as movement activists, Nader and other egalitarians constantly criticize mere "politicians," who supposedly lack courage and shrink from taking principled stands. Activists therefore do not fully appreciate the role of elected officials as go-betweens, as tension reducers, as masters of timing and symbolism, and as people who want everyday life to go on once a particular election or argument is over. Of course they want to stay elected, and they deserve that bit of egoism, because they have glad-handed many thousands of people and listened to an earful to get where they are. Winning an elected office is not the kind of close-in emotional labor that very many people can tolerate unless they enjoy small talk, back patting and endless arguments with people they hardly know, or don't know at all.

Perhaps needless to say, then, there are few moral activists who are also good politicians.

Although most egalitarians think liberal politicians should just stand up for what they believe in, and take the consequences, they are better thought of as the egalitarian activists' negotiators and diplomats within a democratic system. Yes, they should have strong liberal principles, but they also have to know when to do battle and when not to, and when it is time to cut a deal. Their goal is to win the best they think possible for their side at any given moment, and to be back for the next round. The crucial point for egalitarians is this: the liberals among politicians can only prosper when the egalitarian moral activists and their social movements have made better deals possible, either by causing the election of more liberals or by forcing the moderates and conservatives to accept a deal they don't like in order to avoid losing the next election.

This interaction and mutual reinforcement between egalitarian activists and liberal politicians is the key to a new egalitarian movement. Progressive social change depends greatly on social movement organizations and strategic nonviolent actions outside the electoral area, but it requires an electoral dimension as well. Respecting the electoral dimension also requires that activists resist any temptation to take the hard-won democratic gains of the past for granted, or even treat them with contempt. Egalitarians might like liberal politicians better if they thought of them as the defenders of the gains that have been made by egalitarians in the past. It was egalitarians in the nineteenth-century Populist Party, for example, which helped force the direct election of Senators.

Perhaps needless to say, then, there are few moral activists who are also good politicians. The most striking exception is John Lewis, one of the truly great leaders of the early Civil Rights Movement, who stood for principled nonviolence and therefore was ousted as the leader of Student Nonviolent Co-ordinating Committee by Black Power advocates in 1965 when they ran out of patience with cautious white liberals and flawed trade unionists. Lewis recovered from that rejection and spent several years helping to register African-American voters throughout the South. Then he won a seat on the Atlanta city council in 1981 and an uphill battle for Congress in 1986. By 2009 he was one of the most powerful voices of the Democratic Party in the House of Representatives. It is the few people like Lewis who can bridge the gap between social movements and politics.

So what should egalitarian activists do in terms of future elections if and when the issues, circumstances, and candidates seem right? First, they should form Egalitarian Democratic Clubs, which could of course have any name they wished (e.g., Green Democrats, Gay Democrats, Progressive Democrats), but the point is that egalitarianism is the basic value system of the club members. That gives egalitarians an organizational base as well as a distinctive new social identity within the structural pathway to government that is labeled "the Democratic Party." Forming such clubs makes it possible for activists to maintain their sense of separatism and purity while at the same time allowing them to compete within the Democratic Party. There are numerous precedents for such clubs within the party, including liberal and reform clubs in the past, and the conservative Democratic Leadership Council at the present time.

Members of the right wing within the Republican Party follow this strategy of forging a separate social identity. In doing so they have, unfortunately, proven its effectiveness by taking over the party. By joining organizations like the Moral Majority and Christian Coalition, they can define themselves as Christians who have to work out of necessity within the debased confines of the Republican Party. That is, they think of themselves as Christians first and Republicans second, and that is what egalitarians should do: identify themselves primarily as egalitarians and only secondarily as Democrats.

After forming Egalitarian Democrat Clubs, egalitarian activists should find people to run in selected Democratic primaries from precinct to president. They should not simply support eager candidates who come to them with the hope of turning them into campaign workers. They have to create candidates of their own who already are committed to the egalitarian movement and to its alternative economic vision of planning through the market. The candidates have to be responsible to the clubs, or else the candidates naturally will look out for their own self-interest and careers. They should focus on winning on the basis of the program, and make no personal criticisms of their Democratic rivals. Personal attacks on mainstream politicians are a mistake, a self-made trap, for egalitarian insurgents.

In talking about the program, the candidates actually do much more than explain what egalitarians stand for. By discussing such issues as increasing inequality and the abandonment of fairness, and then placing the blame for these conditions on the corporate-conservative coalition and the Republican Party, they help to explain to fellow members of the movement who is "us" and who is "them." They help to create a sense of "we-ness," a new collective identity. As candidates who present a positive program and attack those who oppose it, they are serving as "entrepreneurs of identity," an important part of the job description for any spokesperson in a new social movement.

Since egalitarians are not likely to have the resources to run at all levels in all places, what are the best places to start when a good opportunity arises? One possibility is in Republican-dominated districts where it might be easy to take over moribund Democratic Party structures that do not try to put forward serious candidates. There are now many such House districts that might be ripe for the picking. Winning in Democratic primaries and then facing seemingly invincible Republican incumbents in the regular election may be more useful than it might seem at first glance. For example, when a progressive group in Michigan launched such a grassroots campaign in a Republican district in 1986, with the goal of sending the incumbent a message about his support for Reagan's militaristic foreign policy, their Democratic candidate received 41 percent of the vote, 10 percent higher than the previous Democratic challenger. Such a large vote on the first try would be a wonderful starting point if it could be achieved in the same election year in a number of districts and states where the regular Democrats already had conceded the election to the Republicans.

It also makes sense to run candidates at the congressional level in a few highly Democratic districts, where an egalitarian might have a real chance of winning the regular election if he or she could win the primary. These opportunities might arise when incumbent Democrats leave their seats for one reason for another in districts where grassroots activists have established a strong record through their non-electoral efforts. They would be entering primaries in which there would likely be several candidates splitting the moderate vote. Since the turnout is often low in primaries, a highly organized egalitarian campaign that fully mobilized all of its potential supporters would have some solid possibilities.

What It Takes to Make a Well-Rounded Third-Party Candidate

As for the presidential level, a focus on one well-known activist with good egalitarian credentials might be worthwhile if the campaign was used to develop Egalitarian Democratic

Clubs and other party-transforming activities. Absent such a person, different candidates could be fielded on the same platform in different regions of the country, or in selected states such as New York, Massachusetts, Oregon, and California. That way, the effort could be made without having to raise huge amounts of money.

For example, a John Lewis or some other prominent liberal African-American leader with political experience as an elected official might be able to win the Super Tuesday primaries across the Southern states, thereby heightening the visibility and strengthening the role of African-Americans in the egalitarian wing of the party. It is often overlooked that Jesse Jackson won the most votes overall in this string of same-day primaries when they were first held in 1988, thanks for the most part to the African-American vote. And if enough different presidential candidates were able to win delegates in a range of states, then it might be possible for egalitarian Democrats to have a role in the Democratic National Convention, which has been reduced in recent decades to a ceremonial occasion and media extravaganza. Perhaps the delegates could even play a part in choosing the vice presidential candidate.

Egalitarian candidates invariably will be asked if they are out to win, or if they expect to win, and the answer should be "Yes, but only on our own terms," which means that winning is only worthwhile if voters are endorsing the egalitarian platform and expressing a sense of identification with the egalitarian movement. Thus, there can be no thought of trimming on one or another part of the agreed-upon platform with the hope of squeaking by. Otherwise, the whole political effort loses it sense of collectivity, and turns back into an individualistic contest based on name recognition and personality.

However, once a highly principled campaign has been waged and the egalitarian challengers lose, as most of them surely would the first few times out, then they should congratulate the winners and announce their support for them in the regular election. Then they should return to work in the social movement of their choice. How they vote in the privacy of the polling booth is their own business, of course, but their public stance should be resolutely pro-Democrat.

There has to be the right combination of issues, momentum, and candidates.

If the insurgents are likely to lose, what is the purpose of the exercise? I am sure you know the answers to that question by now, so I only need to list them fairly quickly:

- Insurgent campaigns in Democratic primaries provide an opportunity to introduce new ideas and programs into the political arena at a time and place when the most politically active citizens are paying at least a little bit of attention.

- By defining the group in terms of its opposition to the corporate-conservative coalition, insurgent campaigns help to forge a sense of collective identity, a sense of "we-ness." An egalitarian Democrat identity is needed as an addition to, not a replacement for, the strong social identities that are already held by the various groups in the coalition.

- The reactions of voters to these new policy proposals provide an opportunity to hone and refine them so they better suit the needs of those they are designed to serve.

- Insurgent campaigns provide an opportunity to recruit new activists who are attracted by the new programs.

- Such campaigns provide egalitarian candidates with much-needed experience in the political arena that could come in very handy at a later date, when there is greater sympathy for an egalitarian program. This experience also keeps candidates and their activist supporters from separating themselves from and disparaging the overwhelming number of people who are non-activists.

- Insurgent campaigns are a chance to gauge the degree of support for egalitarian programs. Anything higher than the few tenths of a percent won by left wing third parties in regular elections in recent decades would be a big moral victory.

- If the vote total is high enough, it gives egalitarians leverage with elected Democrats. It should not be forgotten that it was Jesse Jackson's impressive vote totals in Democratic primaries in 1984 and 1988 that earned him access to the White House in the 1990s. Jackson's campaigns were a disappointment and failure in that he was not really interested in building an organization that was independent of his own career. But that doesn't negate the fact that he won more votes in the primaries in 1988 than Gore, which is a big reason why Clinton and Gore were careful to consult with him throughout their years in office. They didn't want him out there running against them.

Nader's Strategies Hurt His Chances for Presidency

As the analysis in this article shows, both through the cross-national and historical evidence on how electoral systems function, and the frank critique of the Nader presidential campaign of 2000, now all too readily forgotten by the hundreds of leading left scholars who backed him, there is a clear and direct strategy that egalitarians could follow in the electoral arena. It involves transforming the Democratic Party through the formation of Egalitarian Democratic Clubs and then making carefully selected entries into the party's primaries, all the while backing liberals as a far better choice in the regular election than any Green or Republican.

If Nader and his energetic forces had been Green or egalitarian Democrats in 2000, running openly in Democratic Party primaries on their "ten key values," which include a commitment to strategic nonviolence, they would have gained some of the legitimacy needed to take advantage of the economic disasters soon visited upon millions of people by the end of the dot.com boom, the Enron scandal, and finally the collapse of the housing bubble and financial markets generally. Instead, Nader and his supporters ignored the structural realities of the electoral system and opted for a strategy that was bound to hurt and anger liberal Democrats, taking the chance that such a strategy might re-energize grassroots groups and force Democratic candidates to take egalitarian issues more seriously.

However, making things worse is not a winning strategy, and many people's lives became more difficult while the Republicans were in office. Moreover, it is not easy to have all the pieces in place for a chance at establishing an egalitarian toehold in the electoral system. There has to be the right combination of issues, momentum, and candidates. That is why the failed campaign by Nader and the Green Party in 2000 was such a waste as well as a political disaster. It squandered political and moral capital that is very hard for egalitarians to accumulate. Nader's refusal to take the results of social science and historical studies seriously called into question his credibility as a political analyst and made him a pariah among leaders of feminist, environmentalist, and civil rights groups. He left many of his followers confused or disillusioned, while at the same time hardening the moralistic sense of superiority of the handful that remained loyal to his causes. The result was division in the progressive ranks that finally was transcended for most egalitarians as the desperate need to replace President George W. Bush became all too apparent.

Note added in 2009: If the top-down financial bailout strategies being pursued by the Obama Administration and its many advisors from Wall Street do not reduce unemployment, end mortgage foreclosures, and provide affordable health care for low-income and middle-income people, the bottom half of American society, and maybe the bottom 60% or 70%, will suffer greatly. If ever there were a time to run on an egalitarian economic platform in Democratic Party primaries, this would seem to be it. But the economic remedies have to be drawn from pragmatic left-liberals such as Dean Baker, Paul Krugman, Robert Kuttner, and Joseph Stiglitz. There has to be "planning through the market" that shapes energy policy as well as a highly progressive income tax on those who make over $100,000 a year, along with a stronger inheritance tax and a tax on all financial transactions on Wall Street, all of which can be readily legislated by a liberal Congress. The simple truth is that the economy could be run much more openly and fairly while being even more productive, but those who now run the system want to hold on to their status, power, and privileges. The issues are not really about economics once the unworkable extremes of non-market economies (socialism) and totally unregulated economies (free-market capitalism) are eliminated from consideration as ideologies. The real issue is power.

4

The Libertarian Party Undermines the Ideas It Advocates

Bruce Bartlett

Historian Bruce Bartlett is an expert on economic policy. He was a domestic policy advisor to President Ronald Reagan and a treasury official under President George H.W. Bush. He is the author of Impostor: How George W. Bush Bankrupted America and Betrayed the Reagan Legacy, *published in 2006.*

Third parties cannot win elections in America because of the Electoral College. The Libertarian party, therefore, merely pulls libertarian-minded people away from the two major parties, weakening the influence of libertarian thinking. Libertarians would do better to form a lobbying group that would push for libertarian ideas, as pro-life and pro-choice groups do. The Libertarian party must disband before libertarian ideas can effectively advance in either the Republican or the Democratic parties.

In a recent column, I discussed the disaffection of libertarians [individuals in favor of liberty and opposed to government intervention] within the conservative coalition, suggesting that many might be more at home on the political left. A number of readers wrote to say that they agreed with my analysis and had left the Republican Party for the Libertarian Party. Among these is former Republican Rep. Bob Barr of Georgia, who officially joined the Libertarians last week [December 2006].

Of course, people are free to do what they want to do, and if they want to join the Libertarians, that's their business. But if their goal is to actually change policy in a libertarian direction, then they are making a big mistake, in my opinion. The Libertarian Party is worse than a waste of time. I believe it has done far more to hamper the advancement of libertarian ideas and policies than it has done to advance them. In my view, it is essential for the Libertarian Party to completely disappear before libertarian ideas will again have political currency.

The Libertarian Party Cannot Win

The basic problem with the Libertarian Party is the same problem faced by all third parties: It cannot win. The reason is that under the Constitution a candidate must win an absolute majority in the all-important Electoral College. It won't do just to have the most votes in a three- or four-way race. You have to have at least 270 electoral votes to win, period.

Theoretically, this is no barrier to third parties at the state and local level. But in practice, if a party cannot win at the presidential level, it is very unlikely to achieve success at lower levels of government. In short, the Electoral College imposes a two-party system on the country that makes it prohibitively difficult for third parties to compete.

Furthermore, to the extent that third parties exist, they invariably hurt the party closest to them ideologically. When Ralph Nader ran for president in 2000 and 2004, for example, he didn't hurt George W. Bush, he hurt Al Gore and John Kerry. Maybe a few of Nader's voters wouldn't have voted at all if he hadn't run, but the vast bulk of his votes came from Gore's and Kerry's totals. Needless to say, Gore and Kerry are certainly closer to Nader generally than the man he helped elect.

Over the years, I have known a great many people who have flirted with the Libertarian Party, but were ultimately turned off by its political impotence and immaturity. C-SPAN runs Libertarian conventions, and viewers can see for themselves how unserious and childish they are. They show that the Libertarian Party is essentially a high-school-level debating club where only one question is ever debated—who is the purest libertarian, and what is the purest libertarian position?

Both major parties have fewer libertarians than they would without the Libertarian Party, meaning that the net result of the party has been to make our government less libertarian.

At times, serious people have tried to get control of the Libertarian Party and make it a viable organization. But in the end, the crazies who like the party just as it is have always run them off. In the process, however, they have also run off millions of voters who have supported libertarian candidates at one time or another. After realizing what a waste of time the Libertarian Party is, many became disengaged from politics and don't vote at all.

The Libertarian Party Drains Libertarians from the Major Parties

The result has been that libertarian-leaning activists have been drawn away from the Republican Party and the Democratic Party by the Libertarian Party, leaving the major parties with fewer libertarians. In other words, both major parties have fewer libertarians than they would without the Libertarian Party, meaning that the net result of the party has been to make our government less libertarian than it would otherwise be.

My conclusion is that for libertarian ideas to advance, the Libertarian Party must go completely out of business. It must cease to exist, period. No more candidates, no more wasted votes and no more disillusioned libertarian activists.

In place of the party, there should arise a new libertarian interest group organized like the National Rifle Association or the various pro- and anti-abortion groups. This new group, whatever it is called, would hire lobbyists, run advertisements and make political contributions to candidates supporting libertarian ideas. It will work with both major parties. It can magnify its influence by creating temporary coalitions on particular issues and being willing to work with elected officials who may hold libertarian positions on only one or a handful of issues. They need not hold libertarian views on every single issue, as the Libertarian Party now demands of those it supports.

I believe that this new organization would be vastly more influential than the party and give libertarian ideas far more potency than they now have. As long as the party continues to exist, unfortunately, it will be an albatross around the necks of small-L libertarians, destroying any political effectiveness they might have. It must die for libertarian ideas to succeed.

5

Protesting the Two-Party System by Voting for Third-Party Candidates

Ron Paul

Ron Paul is a Republican Congressman from Texas. He was the Presidential nominee of the Libertarian Party in 1988. In 2008 he ran for the Republican party presidential nomination; although he won no statewide contests, his candidacy generated a great deal of enthusiasm.

There is no real difference between the two major parties. They both support the status quo of privileged, moneyed interests. Real change—an end to the American world empire or a reduction of the national debt—will not come from the Democrats or Republicans. Therefore, people need to vote for third-party candidates to show their dissatisfaction and to send a message to those in power.

The coverage of the presidential election is designed to be a grand distraction. This is not new, but this year [2008], it's more so than ever.

Pretending that a true difference exists between the two major candidates is a charade of great proportion. Many who help to perpetuate this myth are frequently unaware of what they are doing and believe that significant differences actually do exist. Indeed, on small points there is the appearance of a difference. The real issues, however, are buried in a barrage of

Ron Paul, "Ron Paul Statement to the National Press Club," *Campaign for Liberty*, September 10, 2008.

miscellaneous nonsense and endless pontifications by robotic pundits hired to perpetuate the myth of a campaign of substance.

The Two Parties Are Effectively the Same

The truth is that our two-party system offers no real choice. The real goal of the campaign is to distract people from considering the real issues.

Influential forces, the media, the government, the privileged corporations and moneyed interests see to it that both partys' candidates are acceptable, regardless of the outcome, since they will still be in charge. It's been that way for a long time. [Four-time presidential candidate] George Wallace was not the first to recognize that there's "not a dime's worth of difference" between the two parties. There is, though, a difference between the two major candidates and the candidates on third-party tickets and those running as independents.

This message can be sent to our leaders by not participating in the Great Distraction—the quadrennial campaign and election of an American President without a choice.

The two parties and their candidates have no real disagreements on foreign policy, monetary policy, privacy issues, or the welfare state. They both are willing to abuse the Rule of Law and ignore constitutional restraint on Executive Powers. Neither major party champions free markets and private-property ownership.

Those candidates who represent actual change or disagreement with the status quo are held in check by the two major parties in power, making it very difficult to compete in the pretend democratic process. This is done by making it difficult for third-party candidates to get on the ballots, enter into the debates, raise money, avoid being marginalized, or get fair or actual coverage. A rare celebrity or a wealthy individual can, to a degree, overcome these difficulties.

The system we have today allows a President to be elected by as little as 32% of the American people, with half of those merely voting for the "lesser of two evils". Therefore, as little as 16% actually vote for a president. No wonder when things go wrong, anger explodes. A recent poll shows that 60% of the American people are not happy with the two major candidates this year.

A Vote for a Third-Party Is a Vote Against the Status Quo

This system is driven by the conviction that only a major party candidate can win. Voters become convinced that any other vote is a "wasted" vote. It's time for that conclusion to be challenged and to recognize that the only way not to waste one's vote is to reject the two establishment candidates and join the majority, once called silent, and allow the voices of the people to be heard.

We cannot expect withdrawal of troops from Iraq or the Middle East with either of the two major candidates. Expect continued involvement in Iran, Iraq, Afghanistan, Pakistan and Georgia. Neither hints of a non-interventionist foreign policy. Do not expect to hear the rejection of the policy of supporting the American world empire. There will be no emphasis in protecting privacy and civil liberties and the constant surveillance of the American people. Do not expect any serious attempt to curtail the rapidly expanding national debt. And certainly, there will be no hint of addressing the Federal Reserve System and its cozy relationship with big banks and international corporations and the politicians.

There is only one way that these issues can get the attention they deserve: the silent majority must become the vocal majority.

This message can be sent to our leaders by not participating in the Great Distraction—the quadrennial campaign and election of an American President without a choice. Just think of how much of an edge a Vice President has in this process, and he or she is picked by a single person—the party's nominee. This was never intended by the Constitution.

Recognize Non-Voters, Write-In Voters, and Third-Party Voters

Since a principled non-voter sends a message, we must count them and recognize the message they are sending as well. The non-voters need to hold their own "election" by starting a "League of Non-voters" and explain their principled reasons for opting out of this charade of the presidential elective process. They just might get a bigger membership than anyone would guess.

Write-in votes should not be discouraged, but the electoral officials must be held accountable and make sure the votes are counted. But one must not be naïve and believe that under today's circumstances one has a chance of accomplishing much by a write-in campaign.

My advice—for what it's worth—is to vote! Reject the two candidates who demand perpetuation of the status quo and pick one of the alternatives.

The strongest message can be sent by rejecting the two-party system, which in reality is a one-party system with no possible chance for the changes to occur which are necessary to solve our economic and foreign policy problems. This can be accomplished by voting for one of the non-establishment principled Candidates—[Constitution Party Candidate Chuck] Baldwin, [Libertarian Party Candidate Bob] Barr, [Green Party Candidate Cynthia] McKinney, [Independent Candidate Ralph] Nader, and possibly others (listed alphabetically).

Yes, these individuals do have strong philosophic disagreements on various issues, but they all stand for challenging the status quo—those special interests who control our federal government. And because of this, on the big issues of war, civil liberties, deficits, and the Federal Reserve, they have much in common. People will waste their vote in voting for the lesser of two evils. That can't be stopped overnight, but for us to have an impact we must maximize the total votes of those rejecting the two major candidates.

For me, though, my advice—for what it's worth—is to vote! Reject the two candidates who demand perpetuation of the status quo and pick one of the alternatives that you have the greatest affinity to, based on the other issues.

A huge vote for those running on principle will be a lot more valuable by sending a message that we've had enough and want real change than wasting one's vote on a supposed lesser of two evils.

6

Third Parties in the U.S Cannot Win, But They Are Still Worthwhile

Brian Doherty

Brian Doherty is a senior editor at Reason *magazine and* Reason.com. *He has written for numerous newspapers and magazines, and he frequently contributes to television and radio programs. He is the author of* Radicals for Capitalism: A History of the Modern American Libertarian Movement, *published in 2007.*

It is true that in the United States, third parties cannot win a major election, and they rarely advance their ideological goals. Nonetheless, third parties provide interest and excitement for their members. On those grounds, they are worthwhile.

The next president of the United States will be either a Democrat or Republican. It's a daring prediction, I know. But by sticking with it, I've called every election in my lifetime.

This might make it seem a waste of intellectual effort even to think about third parties. That attitude, though, reduces electoral politics to a purely instrumental role—which isn't necessarily the most illuminating way to think about it.

These days, we have two "third parties" that more or less take seriously certain attitudes implicit within limited factions of the two major ones: the Libertarians for strictly limited

Brian Doherty, "Third Parties, Fifth Rate?" Reason.com, February 12, 2004. Reproduced by permission.

government types who find the GOP too statist, and the Greens for environmentalist/anti-corporate/mega-welfare state types who think the Democrats have sold their souls to monied interests. Of course, neither party has much of a chance of proving "significant" in the 2004 elections, on any level.

Third Parties Are Trapped

Mother Jones recently ran a detailed, thoughtful, and ultimately on-the-one-hand, on-the-other-hand story about the dilemma the Green Party faces in the wake of Ralph Nader, simultaneously the spoiler who hurt their reputation and the only man who got them official ballot status in many states [during his presidential run in 2000].

Ideological third parties are in a pretty inescapable trap in our current electoral system—no coincidence, as the rules are written by, and for, the benefit of, the two major parties.

His spoiler status made lots of possibly sympathetic voters mad at the Greens; but an energetic national campaign provides a very effective recruiting hook and, thanks to ballot-access laws, often the only chance to reach the starting line of elections without expensive and annoying signature drives. It might be, as *Mother Jones* suggests, that concentrating their time and resources on more-winnable local races would increase the Greens' electoral success rate. But election laws as they stand make that an impossible choice for third parties who strive for ballot access.

Ideological third parties are in a pretty inescapable trap in our current electoral system—no coincidence, as the rules are written by, and for the benefit of, the two major parties. Certain huge structural changes—like a return to ballot fusion (in which third parties could declare an acceptable major party candidate their candidate on the ballot as well) or a change to ranked voting (in which you don't just pick one favorite, but list your choices in preference order)—could increase third party clout in our system by eliminating the phony "wasted vote" dilemma. But such changes are obviously wildly unlikely. In our first-past-the-post two-party system, the best a third party can manage on the national or federal congressional level is being a spoiler. (Successes on more local levels seem scarcely more inspirational).

Some people, after all, will only want to vote when they can cast their support publicly behind someone who truly believes what they believe.

There are even more reasons to consider third party candidacy a waste of time. It's quite possible that on lower levels (though not on the presidential level), candidates who would have made ideal Green true believers might capture a Democratic Party nomination, or a staunch libertarian win the hearts of local or state level Republicans. And if libertarian-minded would-be political activists had pursued a Religious Right strategy of doing the party scutwork at the precinct level, thus achieving disproportionate power in the party apparatus, we might have a much more libertarian Republican Party today.

And as others have noted, "greens" (not Greens) have done far better for their ideology in the public arena pursuing strategies other than third-party politics.

Voting Is Not Always About Winning

But to leap from all those truths to the conclusion that third parties ought to pack it in ignores something important: Voting isn't purely an instrumental act. (If it were, and if each individual were striving toward rational maximization, there'd be even less voting than there now is, since any individuals' chance to change the actual outcome of an election is so minimal it's barely worth calculating.) Some people, after all, will only want to vote when they can cast their support publicly behind someone who truly believes what they believe, not just someone who is less awful along their relevant metrics than the only other "real" choice.

In thinking about third parties' role, one is musing about what tens of thousands of *other* people should be doing to further the acceptance of their ideas in a big, complicated, multifaceted world. Once when I was interviewing David Bergland, one of the Libertarian Party's [LP] longtime mainstays (and one of its least successful presidential candidates), I floated by him the idea, popular among libertarians who consider themselves well-suited for real-world struggles, that the LP strategy was a waste of time for the liberty-minded—that it was positively detrimental compared to, say, legal, journalistic, or think-tank activism.

Bergland seethed. Who, he asked, should tell him how he should choose to exert his energies in the defense of liberty? The LP perfectly suited his temperament, style, and choices—but for it, perhaps, he'd practice no ideological activism at all.

People who believe they are having fun actually are having fun; those who assume their vote is swaying the election are just wrong.

That rang true for me. I know for certain that the existence of the [Libertarian] Ron Paul campaign in 1988 helped cement my interest in politics and liberty when I was 20 years old, and that passion remained even when the object of it shifted from presidential elections to writing and reporting. Ideological/political movements—particularly libertarian ones!—should not be centrally planned, with one tendency dominating because the smartest people have decided it's the most efficient or effective. Everyone will have different desires, and different mechanisms will suit them more than others.

Ideological third parties clearly have never been about actually getting candidates into office, unless one is positing (and I know some would have no problem doing so) that everyone involved in them is utterly irrational.

Third Parties Are Enjoyable

It is perhaps best to think of them not as actual engines by which to propel outré political forces into office, or even as necessarily efficient means to spread ideas and influence to the general public, but as a joyous consumption expense—just one more of the many pleasing options to pass the time that quasi-capitalist modernity provides. Perhaps third parties continue to crawl along, trailing electoral failure after electoral failure, even on occasion poisoning those possibly sympathetic toward the ideas they claim to support (see any number of spoiler complaints against Greens and Libertarians), because to the people who want to work on them, they are just exactly what they want to work on. They are fun and fulfilling and meet a consumer need regardless of "effectiveness" as judged by an outsider.

That's worth celebrating in and of itself. I've come to think this is almost certainly the real reason third parties do survive, though publicly advocating personal satisfaction as the reason they are important runs into a "noble lie" dilemma for those who want to see them thrive. After all, if most third party activists were consciously aware of this aspect of the party, would they still feel the same passionate interest in them? On personal reflection, I think the answer could well be yes.

And for those for whom it isn't, well, they will eventually stop concentrating their public-spirited energies on third parties and either drop out of electoral politics altogether (as I did) or move on to the more "rational" choices. But in the meantime, many people will support third parties because they enjoy them. Serious politicos may think this is a dangerously frivolous reason to support those institutions, given the (rare, but not unprecedented) serious effect on elections their existence can have. But that still puts third-party supporters ahead of those who ridiculously assume that their vote might actually sway an election. People who believe that they are having fun actually are having fun; those who assume their vote is swaying the election are just wrong.

Mao [Tse-tung, Communist leader of the People's Republic of China] was right about one thing: Let a thousand flowers bloom. And you don't always let those flowers bloom because they are going to accomplish something practical and vital. All those flowers can also be worth supporting because people enjoy looking at them.

7

The Electoral College Ensures Nationwide, Moderate, and Stable Parties

Peter W. Schramm

Peter W. Schramm is a professor of Political Science at Ashland University and executive director of the John M. Ashbrook Center for Public Affairs. He served during the Ronald Reagan Administration in the Department of Education.

The founding fathers did not intend America to have direct majority rule. Instead, they tried to balance majority power with rationality. The Electoral College system, in which the winner takes all, forces the parties to be ideologically and geographically broad-based and inclusive. This institution therefore makes America's government stable and moderate.

Those who are keen on abolishing the Electoral College in favor of a direct election of the president, are, whether they know it or not, proposing the most radical transformation in our political system that has ever been considered. I am opposed to such transformation for the same reason that I support the Constitution.

Those who make the argument that a simple majority, one man, one vote, as it were, is the fairest system, make the mistake of confusing democracy, or the simple and direct rule of the majority, with good government. When they argue that democracy is subverted by the Electoral College they are mistaken.

Peter W. Schramm, "Is the Electoral College Passé?: No." *Ashbrook Center*, November 16, 2004. Reproduced by permission of the author.

The opponents of the Electoral College confuse means with ends, ignore the logic of the Constitution, have not studied history and are oblivious to the ill effects its abolition would have.

The Constitution Restrains Majority Rule

The framers of the Constitution knew that all previous democracies were short-lived and died violently; they became tyrannies, wherein the unrestrained majorities acted only in their own interests and ignored the rights of the minority. The framers' "new science of politics" sought to avoid this.

The Constitution encourages the people to construct a certain kind of majority, a reasonable majority, a majority that tempers the passions and interests of the people.

While all political authority comes from the people—hence [James] Madison calls this a "popular" regime—the purpose of government according to the Declaration of Independence is to secure the natural rights of each citizen. The purpose of our intricate constitutional architecture—separation of powers, bicameralism, representation, staggered elections, federalism, the Electoral College—is to try to make as certain as possible, knowing that people are not angels, that this be accomplished. The Constitution attempts to combine consent with justice. This is what we mean when we say that the Constitution is a limiting document.

It is self-evident that all these devices depart in one way or another, from simple numerical majoritarianism. For the Constitution, the formation of majorities is not simply a mathematical or quantitative problem.

Why should California have only two U.S. senators, while Wyoming also has two? Why should the election of senators be staggered so that only a third are up for election in any one cycle? Why should there be an independent judiciary?

Why should the president be elected by an Electoral College that is controlled by the states?

The answers revolve around this massive fact: The Constitution encourages the people to construct a certain kind of majority, a reasonable majority, a majority that tempers the passions and interests of the people. The Constitution attempts to create a majority—one could even say many majorities—that is moderate, that is limited and one that will make violating the rights of the minority very difficult. In short, the Constitution is concerned with the *character* of majorities formed.

The Electoral College Is a Moderating Force

The Electoral College is the lynchpin in this constitutional structure. Although Alexander Hamilton admitted that it wasn't perfect, yet he called it "excellent." The framers of the Constitution debated at length how a president should be chosen before settling on the Electoral College.

In large measure because of the Electoral College, each political party is broad-based and moderate.

At the Constitutional Convention they twice defeated a plan to elect the president by direct vote, and also defeated a plan to have Congress elect the president. The latter would violate the separation of powers, while the former would, they argued, lead to what Hamilton called "the little arts of popularity," or what we call demagoguery.

So they crafted the Electoral College. This has come to mean that every four years a temporary legislature in each state is elected by the people, whose sole purpose is to elect a president. It then dissolves, to reappear four years later. In other words we have a democratic election for president, but it is democratic within each state. Yet, within each state, the winner of the popular vote takes all the electoral votes of that state. Citizens in Colorado this month [November 2004] made the right decision to keep a winner-take-all system.

This method not only bolsters federalism, but also encourages and supports a two-party system. In large measure because of the Electoral College, each political party is broad-based and moderate. Each party has to mount a national campaign, state by state, that considers the various different interests of this extended republic. Majorities are built that are both ideologically and geographically broad and moderate. While the two-party system does not eliminate partisanship, it does moderate it.

> *The Electoral College ensures that an elected president would be responsive not to a concentrated majority, but to the nation as a whole.*

Each party is pulled to the center, producing umbrella-like coalitions before an election, rather than after, as happens in the more turbulent regimes of Europe, for example. As a result, we do not have runoffs, as most other democracies do. It forces both parties to practice politics inclusively.

The Electoral College Creates Stability

Nor do we have a radicalized public opinion as the Europeans do. What we have is a system that produces good, constitutional politics, and the kind of stability that no other "popular regime" has ever experienced.

The Electoral College ensures that an elected president would be responsive not to a concentrated majority, but to the nation as a whole. This process is one of the most important safeguards of our democratic form of government. Leave the Electoral College and the Constitution alone.

8

The Electoral College Is Undemocratic and Should Be Abolished

Bradford Plumer

Bradford Plumer is an assistant editor at The New Republic, *where he reports on energy and environmental issues. He also has written for* The American Prospect, Audubon, The Journal of Life Sciences, In These Times, *and* Mother Jones.

The Electoral College is unfair, it has the chance of badly misrepresenting the will of the people, and it gives disproportionate power to a few voters in swing states. Moreover, defenses of the Electoral College are unconvincing. The College does not encourage broad geographical appeal, for example, because candidates tend to refrain from campaigning in states that have few Electoral College votes or in states that typically are aligned with either the Democratic or the Republican party. Abolishing the Electoral College would not cause instability or chaos, but would promote democracy and rationality.

What have [Republican President] Richard Nixon, [Democratic President] Jimmy Carter, [Republican Presidential Candidate] Bob Dole, the U.S. Chamber of Commerce, and the AFL-CIO [a federation of labor unions] all, in their time, agreed on? Answer: Abolishing the Electoral College! They're not alone; according to a Gallup poll in 2000, taken shortly after Al Gore—thanks to the quirks of the Electoral College—

Bradford Plumer, "The Indefensible Electoral College," *Mother Jones Online*, October 8, 2004. Reproduced by permission.

won the popular vote but lost the presidency, over 60 percent of voters would prefer a direct election to the kind we have now. This year [2004] voters can expect another close election in which the popular vote winner could again lose the presidency. And yet, the Electoral College still has its defenders. What gives?

As George C. Edwards III, a professor of political science at Texas A&M University, reminds us in his new book, *Why the Electoral College Is Bad for America*, "The choice of the chief executive must be the people's, and it should rest with none other than them." Fans of the Electoral College usually admit that the current system doesn't quite satisfy this principle. Instead, Edwards notes, they change the subject and tick off all the "advantages" of the electoral college. But even the best-laid defenses of the old system fall apart under close scrutiny. The Electoral College has to go.

The Electoral College Is Dangerous and Unfair

Under the Electoral College system, voters vote not for the president, but for a slate of electors, who in turn elect the president. If you lived in Texas, for instance, and wanted to vote for Kerry, you'd vote for a slate of 34 Democratic electors pledged to Kerry. On the off-chance that those electors won the statewide election, they would go to Congress and Kerry would get 34 electoral votes. Who are the electors? They can be anyone not holding public office. Who picks the electors in the first place? It depends on the state. Sometimes state conventions, sometimes the state party's central committee, sometimes the presidential candidates themselves. Can voters control whom their electors vote for? Not always. Do voters sometimes get confused about the electors and vote for the wrong candidate? Sometimes.

The single best argument *against* the electoral college is what we might call the disaster factor. The American people should consider themselves lucky that the 2000 fiasco was the biggest election crisis in a century; the system allows for much worse. Consider that state legislatures are technically responsible for picking electors, and that those electors could always defy the will of the people. Back in 1960, segregationists in the Louisiana legislature nearly succeeded in replacing the Democratic electors with new electors who would oppose John F. Kennedy. (So that a popular vote for Kennedy would not have actually gone to Kennedy.) In the same vein, "faithless" electors have occasionally refused to vote for their party's candidate and cast a deciding vote for whomever they please. This year, one Republican elector in West Virginia has already pledged not to vote for Bush; imagine if more did the same. Oh, and what if a state sends *two* slates of electors to Congress? It happened in Hawaii in 1960. Luckily, Vice President Richard Nixon, who was presiding over the Senate, validated only his opponent's electors, but he made sure to do so "without establishing a precedent." What if it happened again?

At the most basic level, the Electoral College is unfair to voters.

Perhaps most worrying is the prospect of a tie in the electoral vote. In that case, the election would be thrown to the House of Representatives, where state delegations vote on the president. (The Senate would choose the vice-president.) Because each state casts only one vote, the single representative from Wyoming, representing 500,000 voters, would have as much say as the 55 representatives from California, who represent 35 million voters. Given that many voters vote one party for president and another for Congress, the House's selection can hardly be expected to reflect the will of the people. And if an electoral tie seems unlikely, consider this: In 1968, a shift of just 41,971 votes would have deadlocked the election. In 1976, a tie would have occurred if a mere 5,559 voters in

Ohio and 3,687 voters in Hawaii had voted the other way. The election is only a few swing voters away from catastrophe.

At the most basic level, the Electoral College is unfair to voters. Because of the winner-take-all system in each state, candidates don't spend time in states they know they have no chance of winning, focusing only on the tight races in the "swing" states. During the 2000 campaign, seventeen states didn't see the candidates at all, including Rhode Island and South Carolina, and voters in 25 of the largest media markets didn't get to see a single campaign ad. If anyone has a good argument for putting the fate of the presidency in the hands of a few swing voters in Ohio, they have yet to make it.

Defenses of the Electoral College Are Unconvincing

So much for the charges against the Electoral College. The arguments in favor of the Electoral College are a bit more intricate. Here's a quick list of the favorite defenses—and the counterarguments that undo them.

The founding fathers wanted it that way!—Advocates of the Electoral College often appeal to the wisdom of the founding fathers—after all, they set up the system, presumably they had something just and wise in mind, right? Wrong. History shows that the framers whipped up the Electoral College system in a hurry, with little discussion and less debate. Whatever wisdom the founding fathers had, they sure didn't use it to design presidential elections. At the time, most of the framers were weary after a summer's worth of bickering, and figured that George Washington would be president no matter what, so it wasn't a pressing issue.

Most of the original arguments in favor of an Electoral College system are no longer valid. The Electoral College was partially a concession to slaveholders in the South, who wanted electoral clout without letting their slaves actually vote. (Under the Electoral College, slaves counted towards a state's electoral vote total.) The framers also thought that ordinary people wouldn't have enough information to elect a president, which is not necessarily a concern today.

It protects state interests!—States don't really have coherent "interests," so it's hard to figure out exactly what this means. (Is there something, for instance, that all New Yorkers want purely by virtue of being New Yorkers?) Under the current system, presidents rarely campaign on local issues anyway—when [political science professor] George Edwards analyzed campaign speeches from 1996 and 2000, he found only a handful that even mentioned local issues. And that's as it should be. We have plenty of Congressmen and Senators who cater to local concerns. The president should take a broader view of the national interest, not be beholden to any one state or locale.

Factions already exist—white male voters vote Republican; African-Americans vote Democrat. . . . If our polarized country is a concern, it has little to do with the Electoral College.

It's consistent with federalism!—All history students recall that the Great Compromise of 1787 created the House, which gives power to big populous states, and the Senate, which favors small states. The compromise was just that, a *compromise* meant to keep delegates happy and the Constitution Convention in motion. Nevertheless, the idea that small states need protection has somehow become legitimated over the years, and is used to support the Electoral College—which gives small states disproportionate power in electing a president. But what, pray tell, do small states need protection *from*? It's not as if big states are all ganging up on Wyoming. The fiercest rivalries have always been between regions, like the South and North in the 1800s, or between big states, like California and Texas today. Furthermore, most small states are ignored in presidential campaigns, so it's not clear that the current system is protecting anything.

It protects minorities!—Some college buffs have argued that, since ethnic minorities are concentrated in politically competitive states, the Electoral College forces candidates to pay more attention to minorities. This sounds great, but it's wholly untrue. Most African-Americans, for instance, are concentrated in the South, which has rarely been a "swing" region. Hispanic voters, meanwhile, largely reside in California, Texas, and New York, all uncompetitive states. It's true that Cubans in Florida have benefited wonderfully from the Electoral College, but they represent an extremely narrow interest group. All other minority voters have *less* incentive to vote. It's no surprise that the Electoral College has often enabled presidential candidates to ignore minorities in various states—in the 19th century, for instance, voting rights were poorly enforced in non-competitive states.

George Will's Defense of the Electoral College Is Unconvincing

It makes presidential races more cohesive!—In an August [2004] column for *Newsweek*, [political commentator] George Will argued that the Electoral College somehow makes presidential elections more cohesive. Again, fine in principle, untrue in practice. Will first suggests that the system forces candidates to win a broad swathe of states, rather than just focusing on the most populous regions. But even if that happened, how is that worse than candidates focusing on a few random swing states? Or take Will's claim that the Electoral College system prevents "factions" from "uniting their votes across state lines." What? Factions already exist—white male voters vote Republican; African-Americans vote Democrat; evangelicals vote Republican; atheists vote Democrat. If our polarized country is a concern, it has little to do with the Electoral College.

It gives legitimacy to the winner!—Finally, Will argues that the Electoral College strengthens or legitimizes the winner. For example, Woodrow Wilson won only 41.8 percent of the popular vote, but his 81.9 percent electoral vote victory "produced a strong presidency." This suggests that voters are fools and that the electoral vote total somehow obscures the popular vote total. (If a candidate gets 45 percent of the popular vote, voters aren't going to think he got more than that just because he got 81 percent of the electoral vote total. And even if they do, do we really want a system whose aim is to mislead voters about election results?) Furthermore, there's no real correlation between a strong electoral vote showing and a strong presidency. George H.W. Bush received 426 electoral votes, while Harry Truman received only 303 in 1948 and George W. Bush a mere 271 in 2000. Yet the latter two were undeniably "stronger" presidents in their dealings with Congress. There's also no evidence that an electoral landslide creates a "mandate" for change. The landslides in 1984 and 1972 didn't give [Ronald] Reagan or [Richard] Nixon a mandate for much of anything—indeed, those two presidents got relatively little done in their second terms.

Direct Elections Would Work Fine

Even after all the pro-College arguments have come unraveled, College advocates often insist on digging in their heels and saying that a direct election would be even worse. They're still wrong. Here are the two main arguments leveled against direct elections:

The Electoral College is unfair, outdated, and irrational. The best arguments in favor of it are mostly assertions without much basis in reality.

---

1. The recounts would kill us!—It's true, a nationwide recount would be more nightmarish than, say, tallying up all the

hanging chads [paper fragments created from partially punched vote cards] in Florida. At the same time, we'd be *less* likely to see recounts in a direct election, since the odds that the popular election would be within a slim enough margin of error is smaller than the odds that a "swing" state like Florida would need a recount. Under a direct election, since it usually takes many more votes to sway a race (as opposed to a mere 500 in Florida), there is less incentive for voter fraud, and less reason for candidates to think a recount will change the election. But set aside these arguments for a second and ask: why do so many people fear the recount? If it's such a bad idea to *make sure* that every vote is accurately tallied, then why do we even have elections in the first place?

2. Third parties would run amok!—The ultimate argument against the Electoral College is that it would encourage the rise of third parties. It might. But remember, third parties already play a role in our current system, and have helped swing the election at least four times in the last century—in 1912, 1968, 1992 and 2000. Meanwhile, almost every other office in the country is filled by direct election, and third parties play an extremely small role in those races. There are just too many social and legal obstacles blocking the rise of third parties. Because the Democratic and Republican parties tend to be sprawling coalitions rather than tightly-knit homogenous groups, voters have every incentive to work "within the system". Likewise, in a direct election, the two parties would be more likely to rally their partisans and promote voter turnout, which would in turn *strengthen* the two-party system. And if all else fails, most states have laws limiting third party ballot access anyway. Abolishing the Electoral College won't change that.

It's official: The Electoral College is unfair, outdated, and irrational. The best arguments in favor of it are mostly assertions without much basis in reality. And the arguments against direct elections are spurious at best. It's hard to say this, but Bob Dole was right: Abolish the Electoral College!

9

The Use of Gerrymandering Reduces Accountability of House Incumbents

Juliet Eilperin

Juliet Eilperin is a political and environmental reporter for The Washington Post. *She is the author of* Fight Club Politics: How Partisanship Is Poisoning the House of Representatives, *published in 2006.*

Incumbents in the House of Representatives protect their seats by drawing voting district boundaries along ideological lines so as to benefit their reelection efforts—a process called gerrymandering. The result of gerrymandering is less competition for seats and representatives who are less responsive to the voting public. The process also encourages partisanship, because extreme liberals and conservatives tend to do better than moderates do in gerrymandered districts. The only solution is for the public to realize that gerrymandering is unfair and to force changes through legislative action.

Tom DeLay has fallen, but his handiwork remains—32 Texas congressional districts drawn to guarantee Republican dominance of the state's House delegation. In 2003, at the urging of then-House Majority Leader DeLay, the Texas state legislature redrew the state's political map, an unprecedented gambit that cost five incumbent Democrats their seats in 2004 (four lost in the general election and one retired, while a sixth

Juliet Eilperin, "The Gerrymander That Ate America," Slate.com, April 17, 2006. Reprinted with permission.

switched parties). The map also guaranteed safe seats for almost everyone: The only Texas Republican who would have faced a tight House race in 2006 was DeLay himself. DeLay resigned, of course, to deal with an indictment stemming from the redistricting effort.

Democratic lawyers—and some less partisan types—petitioned the Supreme Court to overturn the Texas redistricting, hoping to persuade the justices that this particularly brazen district-rigging is unconstitutional. The court heard arguments in the case on March 1 [2006]. Many of the plaintiffs would like the court to set some overarching national standards for divvying up the nation's 435 House seats each decade. At the moment each state fends for itself, with varying degrees of success: Some state legislatures handle the job while others rely on independent commissions.

Everyone Agrees Gerrymandering Is Bad

It's hard to find a defender of the current process: It's engineered to favor not only incumbents, but also typically the most ideological ones who derive their power from pandering to party extremists. House incumbents seeking re-election now have a 98 percent chance of winning, up from the lower 90s in the 1990s. It's a system in which party operatives manipulate sophisticated computer software to maximum effect, shuffling voters across district boundaries to guarantee their candidates have the best chance of winning election every two years.

"As a mapmaker, I can have more of an impact on an election than a campaign, than a candidate," says Republican consultant David Winston, who drew House seats for the GOP after the 1990 U.S. Census. "When I, as a mapmaker, have more of an impact on an election than the voters, the system is out of whack."

Even former House Speaker Newt Gingrich, R-Ga., who once embraced such tactics as a key to helping his party take control of Congress, now backs any redistricting reform plan that involves "citizens who do not have an interest in maximizing [political] leverage." Under the current system, Gingrich reasons, Democrats "get to rip off the public in the states where they control and protect their incumbents, and we get to rip off the public in the states we control and protect our incumbents, so the public gets ripped off in both circumstances. . . . In the long run, there's a downward spiral of isolation."

But the New Jersey process has a loophole: If the two parties collude *they can draw a map that protects all the incumbents and outvote the tiebreaker.*

Both partisans and nonpartisans agree congressional elections are a mess. So, what should be done about it? Most congressional experts agree on what a fair system would look like: It would limit redistricting to once a decade in order to reflect the latest population figures. It would place a priority on fostering competitiveness, ensuring minority representation, creating geographically compact districts, and achieving a congressional delegation that reflects the state's overall political balance.

Efforts to Fix the System Have Failed

Is this even possible? There have been some sincere, but unsuccessful, efforts to try. Just last fall voters in California and Ohio considered proposals to create independent redistricting panels, but they rejected both of them by wide margins. In each case members of one party saw the proposal as benefiting the rival party: California Democrats believed Gov. Arnold Schwarzenegger's plan to put three retired judges in charge of redistricting would help the GOP, while Ohio Republicans saw a plan to create an independent citizen's commission as favoring Democrats.

New Jersey has made the boldest effort. It has a redistricting plan that seems perfect on paper but turns out to suffer from an unanticipated fatal flaw. The Garden State has a bipartisan redistricting commission equally divided between the two parties. It is chaired by an impartial tiebreaker—historically, a professor from Rutgers or Princeton University. Each party drafts its own map. Whichever map wins a majority is approved. Both parties thus have an incentive to court the tiebreaking chairman, encouraging them to draw a map that reflects the state's true political leanings.

It's unlikely that members of Congress will push for redistricting reform, because they're the people who benefit the most from the status quo.

But the New Jersey process has a loophole: If the two parties *collude* they can draw a map that protects all the incumbents and outvote the tiebreaker. That's what happened after the 2000 census. The GOP wanted to protect its six incumbents, while Democrats wanted to protect their seven seats. The two parties came up with their incumbent-protection plan and outvoted the tiebreaker, Rutgers University political science professor Allen Rosenthal. It was a bipartisan solution to be sure, but one that protected politicians' interests rather than voters'.

Incumbents Block Solutions

But there *is* a perfect system out there. Sam Hirsch, a D.C. election lawyer who represents lots of Democrats, has drafted a state constitutional amendment, loosely modeled on the New Jersey system, that would keep politicians involved in redistricting while ensuring that the final map would reflect prevailing political opinion. Under Hirsch's plan, the tiebreaking chairman would be almost a redistricting dictator. He would have more votes than all the other members combined, which would block the kind of bipartisan gerrymander that happened in New Jersey. At the same time it would keep politicians involved in the process, allowing them to provide expertise about campaigning and the electoral nature of individual districts.

Americans will be left with the same dismal system . . . until they realize that the problem in Congress isn't just the politicians, but also the process that put them in office.

This process would produce at least two immediate results: It would create more seats with competitive general-election contests, and it would give aspiring politicians an incentive to move a little closer to the political center. That might foster a more meaningful dialogue on Capitol Hill, by reducing the echo-chamber effect that now exists between House members and their like-minded constituents in their Republican- or Democratic-leaning seats.

It's unlikely that members of Congress will push for redistricting reform, because they're the people who benefit the most from the status quo. Rep. John Tanner, a centrist Democrat from Tennessee, introduced legislation nearly a year ago that would establish independent redistricting commissions with independent tiebreakers. It has 46 co-sponsors at the moment, only two of whom are Republican. The companion bill in the Senate has only one sponsor, its author, Tim Johnson, D-S.D.

Unfortunately for Tanner and Hirsch, though many Americans have become increasingly frustrated with Congress, as shown by recent polls, they have yet to recognize how election-proof districts have made lawmakers less accountable to voters and more inclined to fight petty partisan battles. The defeat of the California and Ohio redistricting measures proves how easy it is for entrenched political interests to block change.

The Supreme Court is also unlikely to come to the aid of the reformers. Even if it does throw out DeLay's Texas House map, it is likely to issue the narrowest possible ruling, one that leaves plenty of room for political and partisan redistricting. Americans will be left with the same dismal system, which they will keep until they realize that the problem in Congress isn't just the politicians, but also the process that put them in office.

10

Both Parties Use the Filibuster to Block the Will of the People

David Swanson

David Swanson is a reporter, communications director, and activist. He is the author of Daybreak: Undoing the Imperial Presidency and Forming a More Perfect Union, *published in 2009.*

The filibuster—the use of obstructional tactics such as long speeches to delay or prevent legislative action—is an undemocratic legislative tool. It allows senators representing a small minority of the country to block the majority will. The Senate, which enacts its own rules of conduct, should abolish the practice. At the very least, the Senate should change the rule that allows the breaking of a filibuster from a three-fifths vote to a simple majority vote.

Trying to squeeze any sort of peace on earth out of our government in Washington has been a steep uphill climb for years. For the most part we no longer have representatives in Congress, because of the corruption of money, the weakness of the media, and the strength of parties. There are not 535 opinions on Capitol Hill on truly important matters, but 2. Our supposed representatives work for their party leaders, not for us. Luckily, one of the two parties claims to want to work for us.

David Swanson, "2009: Year of the Filibuster," DavidSwanson.org, December 24, 2008. Reproduced by permission.

When the Democrats were in the minority and out of the White House, they told us they wanted to work for us but needed to be in the majority. So, in 2006, we put them there. Then they told us that they really wished they could work for us but they needed bigger majorities and the White House. So, in 2008, we gave them those things, and largely deprived them of two key excuses for inaction. We took away the veto excuse and came very close to taking away the filibuster excuse, and—in fact—the filibuster excuse could be taken away completely if the Democrats didn't want to keep it around.

This is not to say that either excuse was ever sensible. The two most important things the 110th Congress refused to do (ceasing to fund illegal wars, and impeaching war criminals) did not require passing legislation, so filibusters and vetoes were not relevant. But the Democrats in Congress, and the Republicans, and the media, and the White House all pretended that wars could only be ended by legislation, so the excuses for not passing legislation loomed large. The veto excuse will be gone on January 20th [2009, when Barack Obama became president]. The filibuster excuse could be gone by January 6th if Senator Harry Reid [the Majority Leader] wanted it gone.

The Filibuster Is Anti-Democratic

The filibuster excuse works like this. Any 41 senators can vote No on "cloture", that is on bringing a bill to a vote, and that bill will never come to a vote, and anything the House of Representatives has done won't matter. Any of the other 59 senators, the 435 House members, the president, the vice president, television pundits, and newspaper reporters can blame the threat of filibuster for anything they fail to do.

Now, the Senate itself is and always has been and was intended to be an anti-democratic institution. It serves no purpose that is not or could not be more democratically accomplished by the House alone. The Senate should simply be eliminated by Constitutional Amendment. But the filibuster is the most anti-democratic tool of the Senate, and can be eliminated without touching the Constitution, which does not mention it. If you take 41 senators from the 21 smallest states, you can block any legislation with a group of multimillionaires elected by 11.2 percent of the American public. That fact is a national disgrace that should be remedied as quickly as possible.

Were the Democrats serious about eliminating the filibuster excuse, they would either take every step possible to get 60 senators into their caucus, or they would change the rules requiring 60 senators for cloture.

The filibuster was created by accident when the Senate eliminated a seemingly redundant practice of voting on whether to vote. Senators then discovered, after a half-century of surviving just fine without the filibuster, that they could block votes by talking forever. In 1917 the Senate created a rule allowing a vote by two-thirds of those voting, to end a filibuster. In 1949 they changed the rule to require two-thirds of the entire Senate membership. In 1959 they changed it back. And in 1975 they changed the rule to allow three-fifths of the Senators sworn into office to end a filibuster and force a vote. Filibustering no longer requires giving long speeches. It only requires threatening to do so. The use of such threats has exploded over the past 10 years, dominating the decision-making process of our government and effectively eliminating the possibility of truly populist or progressive legislation emerging from Congress. This has happened at the same time that the forces of money, media, and party have led the Democrats in both houses to view the filibuster excuse as highly desirable, rather than as an impediment.

Democrats Could Easily Eliminate the Filibuster

Were the Democrats serious about eliminating the filibuster excuse, they would either take every step possible to get 60 senators into their caucus, or they would change the rule requiring 60 senators for cloture. Possible steps to reach that magic number of 60 would include ensuring the closest thing possible at this point to honest and verifiable outcomes in the [disputed] Minnesota senate election and every other senate election of this past November [2008], immediately seating replacement senators for [former senator, now President Barack] Obama, [former senator, now vice-President Joe] Biden, and Democrats appointed and confirmed for other offices, appointing Republican senators from states with Democratic governors to key jobs in the Obama administration and immediately seating their replacements, and providing Washington, D.C., with a House member and two senators (this last approach changing the magic number to 61 and potentially providing the 60th and 61st Democrats). Simpler and more certain would be simply changing the rule, specifically Senate Rule 22, which reads in part:

> 'Is it the sense of the Senate that the debate shall be brought to a close?' And if that question shall be decided in the affirmative by three-fifths of the Senators duly chosen and sworn—except on a measure or motion to amend the Senate rules, in which case the necessary affirmative vote shall be two-thirds of the Senators present and voting—then said measure, motion, or other matter pending before the Senate, or the unfinished business, shall be the unfinished business to the exclusion of all other business until disposed of.

A Simple Majority Could End the Filibuster

This would seem to suggest that it takes 60 senators to block a filibuster and 66 senators (if 100 are present, otherwise fewer) to end the power of 60 senators to block filibusters. But that's not the whole story. [Journalist] William Greider recently explained:

> In 1975 the filibuster issue was revived by post-Watergate Democrats frustrated in their efforts to enact popular reform legislation like campaign finance laws. Senator James Allen of Alabama, the most conservative Democrat in the Senate and a skillful parliamentary player, blocked them with a series of filibusters. Liberals were fed up with his delaying tactics. Senator Walter Mondale pushed a campaign to reduce the threshold from sixty-seven votes to a simple majority of fifty-one. In a parliamentary sleight of hand, the liberals broke Allen's filibuster by a majority vote, thus evading the sixty-seven-vote rule. (Senate rules say you can't change the rules without a cloture vote, but the Constitution says the Senate sets its own rules. As a practical matter, that means the majority can prevail whenever it decides to force the issue.) In 1975 the presiding officer during the debate, Vice President [Nelson] Rockefeller, first ruled with the liberals on a motion to declare Senator Allen out of order. When Allen appealed the "ruling of the chair" to the full Senate, the majority voted him down. Nervous Senate leaders, aware they were losing the precedent, offered a compromise. Henceforth, the cloture rule would require only sixty votes to stop a filibuster.

If the Democrats choose to keep the filibuster excuse around, our job will be to overwhelm them and the media with our refusal to believe it.

If Vice President Biden's assistance appears needed for this, it can wait until January 21st [2009, when President Obama takes office.] If it waits longer than that, the credibility of the filibuster excuse will collapse, because the Democrats will be publicly admitting that they prefer to keep that excuse around.

If the [2008] Minnesota election remains undecided, cloture may require one fewer vote under current rules, but the Democrats will have one fewer senator. The outcome of that race will only be decisive if the Democrats refuse to change the filibuster rule and pursue other attempts to achieve a caucus able to vote for cloture. [Note: In July 2009, Al Franken for the Democratic-Farmer-Labor Party was sworn in as Minnesota senator.]

The People Should Refuse to Accept the Filibuster Excuse

If, through one means or another, the Democrats eliminate the filibuster excuse, our job will be to organize and agitate immediately to take full advantage of this rare opportunity for actual representative government. Greider proposes reducing to 55 percent of the Senate the number of senators needed for cloture. I propose reducing it to 50 percent plus one. Either way, nobody is proposing that a minority be empowered to decide anything, only that a majority finally be permitted to (even to the extent allowed by an anti-democratic body like the U.S. Senate in which both Wyoming and California have the same number of senators). Should that happen, all I can say to Wall Street and the military industrial complex is: get ready to be shocked and awed!

If the Democrats choose to keep the filibuster excuse around, our job will be to overwhelm them and the media with our refusal to believe it. Yes, we'll also want to lobby for peace, justice, jobs, green energy, and health care. But we'll never get them unless we insist on pressuring the Senate on this seemingly arcane little matter of passing bills, or what we might call a campaign for "No taxation without representation."

11

The Filibuster Prevents Heated Party Politics

Jim DiPeso

Jim DiPeso is the policy director for Republicans for Environmental Protection. He regularly writes about environmental issues from a Republican perspective at www.the dailygreen.com.

The filibuster puts a check on one-party power. As such, it can slow down or prevent abuses. The filibuster might, for example, be a good way to stop Democrats from using environmental legislation as an excuse for unrestricted federal spending on government programs that benefit a particular congressional district but whose costs are spread among all taxpayers (i.e., pork-barrel projects).

Democrats are effervescing over the possibility that they will win enough Senate seats on Tuesday [November 4, 2008] to have 60 votes, a "filibuster-proof" majority.

Well, it's not that simple. Issues drive the dynamics of each filibuster. It's not a given that every Democrat would vote to shut down every Republican filibuster every time. Or vice versa, if the shoe were on the other foot.

But with one party holding 60 or more votes, the filibuster would be in a weakened state. And that is not necessarily a good thing. Here's to the defense of the filibuster. Not because it is all the leverage that Republicans may have in a town awash in blue [the color of the Democrats]. Because filibusters are a check on excess. And that's good for both parties.

Jim DiPeso, "Three Cheers for Filibusters," thedailygreen.com, November 2, 2008. Reproduced by permission.

The Senate Cools Political Passions

A story, possibly apocryphal, has it that shortly after the Constitutional Convention, Thomas Jefferson was having coffee with George Washington. Jefferson asked why the convention had created the Senate. Washington asked Jefferson why he had just poured his coffee into a saucer. To cool it, Jefferson replied. Exactly why Congress needs a Senate, Washington responded.

The Senate's mission to cool political passions and guard against poorly considered legislation has given rise to institutional traditions that may seem peculiar to Americans and rather baroque to people who live in parliamentary democracies.

One of those traditions is unlimited debate. Until 1917, the tradition was unfettered. That year, the Senate adopted a "cloture" rule requiring a two-thirds vote to end debate. The cloture threshold was cut to three-fifths in 1975. Today, a supermajority of 60 votes is necessary to end a filibuster.

The filibuster entered popular culture in the 1939 film, "Mr. Smith Goes to Washington." The filibusterer, played by Jimmy Stewart, was a hero unmasking corruption.

In real life, filibusterers often are cast as villainous obstructionists. Think [South Carolina Senator] Strom Thurmond and his record-long 24-hour filibuster against civil rights legislation in 1957.

But in 2005, a filibuster prevented Ted Stevens from using defense appropriations legislation to open the Arctic National Wildlife Refuge to oil drilling. A little obstruction can be a good thing, when strong majorities tempt partisans to overreach and abuse their power.

The Filibuster Can Put a Check on Corruption

Now, some of my progressive friends may think that liberals are high-minded people who are immune to the temptations of power that roil human nature. Waxing in exuberance, some believe that after Tuesday [Election Day], the Age of Aquarius will commence, the lion will lie down with the lamb, and Congress will morph into an enduring temple of decency, justice, and humanity.

A Senate that is equipped to carry out its constitutional mission to cool the House's passions would be positioned to . . . prevent America's first national climate legislation from turning into another DC goody bag.

But put down the utopia lollipop for a moment and indulge me in a plausible scenario. The economy notwithstanding, climate change is the biggest long-term issue that we face. We have to get it right and the buy-in to the solution must be broad. As Barack Obama himself said on the *Daily Show* last week [October 2008], it can't be "one party trying to dictate a solution to the problem."

Suppose that the House passes a climate cap-and-trade bill next year. Hundreds of billions of dollars of revenue from auctioning emissions allowances are hanging out there like candy.

Instead of allocating the money to worthwhile endeavors—rebates for hard-pressed energy consumers or renewable energy research, for example—unrestrained House partisans yield to temptation. They decide to splash out auction revenues on porky wheezes that would add little value to the commonweal, but generate fawning press coverage in their districts and heap rewards on their campaign contributors. In the name of creating jobs, of course. The bill passes on a party-line vote.

A Senate that is equipped to carry out its constitutional mission to cool the House's passions would be positioned to slow the legislation down, fix it, and prevent America's first national climate legislation from turning into another DC goody bag. A Senate that is not so equipped may not.

I'm not saying that will happen. I'm just saying that a filibuster-proof Senate is generally not a good thing, for either side of the aisle.

As Huck Finn said: "Overreaching don't pay."

Organizations to Contact

The editors have compiled the following list of organizations concerned with the issues debated in this book. The descriptions are derived from materials provided by the organizations. All have publications or information available for interested readers. The list was compiled on the date of publication of the present volume; the information provided here may change. Readers need to remember that many organizations take several weeks or longer to respond to inquiries.

American Enterprise Institute for Public Policy Research (AEI)
1150 17th St. NW, Washington, DC 20036
(202) 862-5800
Web site: www.aei.org

AEI is a conservative research and education organization that studies national and international issues and conducts political and public opinion studies. It is committed to expanding liberty, increasing individual opportunity, and strengthening free enterprise. The institute publishes monthly periodicals, *American Enterprise* and *AEI Economist*; the bimonthly *Public Opinion*; and books about America's political system, such as *Better Parties, Better Government: A Realistic Program for Campaign Finance Reform*.

Association of Community Organizers for Reform Now (ACORN)
National & Legislative Office, 739 8th St. SE
Washington, DC 20003
(877) 552-2676 • fax: (202) 546-2483
e-mail: natacorndc@acorn.org
Web site: www.acorn.org

ACORN, the nation's largest grassroots community organization for low- and moderate-income people, is a nonprofit, nonpartisan social justice organization. ACORN organizes advocacy campaigns concerned with issues such as minimum wage and predatory lending, provides members with financial services including tax preparation advice, and is involved in extensive voter registration drives. The ACORN Web site features news releases about various topics, such as voter registration, as well as reports, including *Pennsylvania ACORN and Project Vote Election Administration Action Agenda.*

Brookings Institution
1775 Massachusetts Ave. NW, Washington, DC   20036-2188
(202) 797-6000
e-mail: communications@brookings.edu
Web site: www.brookings.edu

The Brookings Institution, founded in 1927, is a liberal think tank that conducts research and education on foreign policy, economics, government, and the social sciences. It publishes the quarterly *Brookings Review*, the biannual *Brookings Papers on Economic Activity*, and various books, including *Election Fraud: Detecting and Deterring Electoral Manipulation.*

Cato Institute
1000 Massachusetts Ave. NW, Washington, DC   20001-5403
(202) 842-0200 • fax: (202) 842-3490
Web site: www.cato.org

The Cato Institute is a libertarian public policy research foundation dedicated to increasing the understanding of policies based on the principles of limited government, free markets, individual liberty, and peace. It publishes the *Cato Journal*; the *Cato Policy Analysis*, a bimonthly newsletter; *Cato Policy Review*; and downloadable papers such as *The Libertarian Vote.*

Center for American Progress Action Fund
1333 H St. NW, 10th Fl., Washington, DC   20005
(202) 682-1611
e-mail: progress@americanprogressaction.org
Web site: www.americanprogressaction.org

The Center for American Progress Action Fund is a progressive think tank that aims to improve the lives of Americans through advocacy, grassroots organization, and partnerships with other progressive leaders. The organization publishes several newsletters, including the daily *The Progress Report*, and the organization's Web site hosts several policy blogs, including *The Wonk Room*, *Think Progress*, and *Yglesias*.

Democratic National Committee (DNC)

430 S Capitol St. SE, Washington, DC   20003
(202) 863-8000
Web site: www.democrats.org

The Democratic National Committee is the principle organization governing the Democratic Party, one of the two main political parties in the United States. The Web site includes the party platform, press releases, news articles, radio addresses, and other articles and publications.

Green Party of the United States

PO Box 57065, Washington, DC   20037
(202) 319-7191 • fax: (888) 289-5260
e-mail: info@gp.org
Web site: www.gp.org

The Green Party of the United States is a political party dedicated to environmental and social justice issues and to grassroots activism. The party participates in local as well as national elections. The organization's Web site includes the party platform, press releases, and news articles. The Green Party publishes a quarterly newspaper, *The Green Pages*, and an e-newsletter, *Greenline*.

Heritage Foundation

214 Massachusetts Ave. NE, Washington, DC   20002
(202) 546-4400 • fax: (202) 546-8328
e-mail: info@heritage.org
Web site: www.heritage.org

The Heritage Foundation is a conservative public policy research institute dedicated to the principles of free, competitive enterprise, limited government, and individual liberty. Its scholars write about various topics, including politics and the party system. Among its publications are the periodic *Backgrounder* and the monthly *Policy Review*.

League of Women Voters

1730 M St. NW, Suite 1000, Washington, DC   20036-4508
(202) 429-1965 • fax: (202) 429-0854
Web site: www.lwv.org

The League of Women Voters is a nonpartisan political organization that works to improve the U.S. government and to influence public policies through citizen education and advocacy. The organization has sponsored many U.S. presidential debates. The League publishes a magazine, *The National Voter*, and an electronic newsletter, *The LeaguE-voice*. The Web site includes a collection of streaming videos, including a video archive of presidential debates.

Libertarian Party

2600 Virginia Ave. NW, Suite 200, Washington, DC   20037
(202) 333-0008 • fax: (202) 333-0072
e-mail: info@lp.org
Web site: www.lp.org

The Libertarian Party is an American political party dedicated to liberty, enterprise, and personal responsibility. The organization's Web site includes the party platform, news updates, and information about the party.

Project Vote Smart (PVS)

One Common Ground, Philipsburg, MT   59858
(888) 868-3762
Web site: www.votesmart.org

Project Vote Smart is a nonprofit, nonpartisan research organization that collects and distributes information about candidates for public office in the United States. Information is distributed via the organization's Web site, a toll-free phone number, and print publications. The project's two major publications are *The Voter's Self-Defense Manual* and *The Reporter's Source Book*. Both are published every two years for each national election.

Reason Foundation
3415 S Sepulveda Blvd., Suite 400, Los Angeles, CA   90034
(310) 391-2245
Web site: www.reason.org

The Reason Foundation promotes individual freedoms and free-market principles. It contends that the United States should avoid the extremes of isolationism and interventionism in its foreign policy. Publications include the monthly *Reason* magazine (as well as Web only content at *Reason Online*), newsletters, research reports, and books.

Republican National Committee
310 First St., Washington, DC   20003
(202) 863-8500 • fax: (202) 863-8820
e-mail: info@gop.com
Web site: www.gop.com

The Republican National Committee is the principle organization governing the Republican Party, one of the two main political parties in the United States. The organization's Web site features the party platform, news articles, and other articles and publications.

Voter Information Services (VIS)
PO Box 649, Reading, MA   01867-0403
(781) 640-2152
e-mail: info@vis.org
Web site: www.vis.org

VIS is a nonpartisan, nonprofit organization dedicated to helping interested citizens learn about the effects of the federal laws enacted by the U.S. Congress and the role of the individual members of Congress in the legislative process. The organization publishes Congressional Report Cards, which show how the positions of each member of Congress match the positions of various advocacy groups.

Bibliography

Books

Ronald
Brownstein

The Second Civil War: Holy Extreme Partisanship Has Paralyzed Washington and Polarized America. London: Penguin Press, 2007.

Brian Doherty

Radicals for Capitalism: A Freewheeling History of the Modern American Libertarian Movement. New York: Public Affairs, 2007.

George C.
Edwards III

Why the Electoral College Is Bad for America. New Haven, CT: Yale University Press, 2004.

Juliet Eilperin

Fight Club Politics: How Partisanship Is Poisoning the House of Representatives. Lanham, MD: Rowman & Littlefield, 2006.

Morris P. Fiorina,
Samuel J. Abrams,
and Jeremy C.
Pope

Culture War?: The Myth of a Polarized America, 2nd ed. Upper Saddle River, NJ: Longman, 2005.

John Clifford
Green and Paul S.
Herrnson

Responsible Partisanship?: The Evolution of American Political Parties Since 1950. Lawrence, KS: University Press of Kansas, 2002.

Howie Hawkins

Independent Politics: The Green Party Strategy Debate. Chicago: Haymarket Books, 2006.

Paul S. Herrnson and John Clifford Green, eds.
Multiparty Politics in America: Prospects and Performance, 2nd ed.. Lanham, MD: Rowman & Littlefield, 2002.

Thomas E. Mann and Bruce E. Cain, eds.
Party Lines: Competition, Partisanship, and Congressional Redistricting. Washington, DC: Brookings Institution Press, 2005.

Nolan McCarty, Keith T. Poole, and Howard Rosenthal
Polarized America: The Dance of Ideology and Unequal Riches. Cambridge, MA: MIT Press, 2006.

Ralph Nader
The Good Fight: Declare Your Independence and Close the Democracy Gap. New York: HarperCollins, 2004.

Ronald B. Rapoport and Walter J. Stone
Three's a Crowd: The Dynamic of Third Parties, Ross Perot, and Republican Resurgence. Ann Arbor, MI: University of Michigan Press, 2005.

Nancy L. Rosenblum
On the Side of the Angels: An Appreciation of Parties and Partisanship. Princeton, NJ: Princeton University Press, 2008.

Tara Ross
Enlightened Democracy: The Case for the Electoral College. Dallas: Colonial Press, 2004.

Ryan Sager   *The Elephant in the Room:*
                           Evangelicals, Libertarians, and the
                           Battle to Control the Republican Party.
                           Hoboken, NJ: John Wiley & Sons,
                           2006.

Douglas Schoen   *Declaring Independence: The*
                           Beginning of the End of the Two-Party
                           System. New York: Random House,
                           2008.

Micah L. Sifry   *Spoiling for a Fight: Third-Party*
                           Politics in America. New York:
                           Routledge, 2003.

Barbara Sinclair   *Party Wars: Polarization and the*
                           Politics of National Policy Making.
                           Norman, OK: University of
                           Oklahoma Press, 2006.

Steven S. Smith   *Party Influence in Congress.* New
                           York: Cambridge University Press,
                           2007.

Gregory J. Wawro   *Filibuster: Obstruction and*
and Eric Schickler   *Lawmaking in the U.S. Senate.*
                           Princeton, NJ: Princeton University
                           Press, 2006.

Periodicals

Radley Balko   "A Rigged System," *Reason Online,*
                           November 5, 2008.

Naftali Bendavid   "Partisan Divide Haunts Obama's
                           Push on Policy," *Wall Street Journal,*
                           February 8, 2009.

Ari Berman   "Partisanship Isn't a Dirty Word,"
                    The Nation, January 27, 2009.

Shamus Cooke   "Dissecting the US Two-Party
                    System," *Peace, Earth, and Justice
                    News*, December 24, 2007.

Economist.com   "A Third Party Threat," May 12,
                    2009.

Amy Farnsworth,   "Three's a Crowd—A History of
Linda Seid   Third-Party Campaigns," *Boston.com*,
Frembes, and   January 16, 2008.
Jason Tuohey

Henry Farrell   "Can Partisanship Save Citizenship?"
                    The American Prospect, December 31,
                    2008.

Joshua Green   "Surprise Party," *The Atlantic*,
                    January–February 2007.

William Greider   "Radical to the Root: A Talk with
                    David Cobb, the Green Presidential
                    Candidate," *The Nation*, December 7,
                    2004.

David   "How the Filibuster Became the
Herszenhorn   Rule," *New York Times*, December 7,
                    2007.

Janet Hook   "Ron Paul Urges Supporters to Vote
                    for a Third-Party Candidate," *Los
                    Angeles Times*, September 11, 2008.

Michael Kinsley   "Libertarians Rising," *Time*, October
                    18, 2007.

Ezra Klein   "The Myth of Bipartisanship," *The American Prospect*, February 9, 2009.

Herbert G. Klein   "Nobody Wins When Partisanship Dominates Politics," *The American Prospect*, October 24, 2006.

Yuval Levin   "Partisanship Is Good," *Newsweek*, February 14, 2009.

Kathryn Jean Lopez   "Fight Club: Washington Needs Partisanship," *National Review Online*, January 28, 2006.

Michael McDonald   "Re-Redistricting Redux," *The American Prospect*, March 6, 2006.

Seema Mehta   "Ralph Nader Decries Country's 'Two-Party Dictatorship,'" *Los Angeles Times*, September 27, 2008.

John Nichols   "Greens Hear Nader, McKinney and Ponder the Politics of 2008," *The Nation*, July 15, 2007.

Timothy Noah   "America's Worst College," *Slate.com*, August 11, 2004.

Katie Paul   "McKinney Goes Green," *Newsweek*, July 15, 2008.

Eleanor Randolph   "Going, Going, Not Gone," *New York Times*, February 26, 2008.

David Lewis Schaeffer   "Don't Mess With the Electoral College," *Wall Street Journal*, July 12, 2008.

Stephanie Simon   "After Initial Success, Electoral College Foes Set Sights on Higher Peaks," *Wall Street Journal*, March 28, 2009.

Justin Soutar   "The Two-Party System: A Catastrophic Failure," *Intellectual Conservative*, August 30, 2007.

Jacob Sullum   "Felonious Advocacy," *Reason Online*, April 1, 2009.

Abigail Thernstrom   "Gerrymandering Democratic Votes," *Forbes.com*, October 23, 2008.

Evan Thomas   "The Closing of the American Mind," *Newsweek*, December 31, 2007–January 7, 2008.

Nathan Thornburgh   "Can the Libertarians Go Mainstream?" *Times Online*, May 21, 2008.

David Weigl   "Bob Barr Talks," *Reason*, November 2008.

Matthew Yglesias   "The Case for Polarization," *The Atlantic*, December 28, 2007. http://matthewyglesias.theatlantic.com.

Index

A

Afghanistan war, 43
African Americans, 12, 15, 29, 32, 60
American Enterprise Institute for Public Policy Research, 7
American Labor Party, 20
American Political Association, 11
Arctic National Wildlife Refuge, 78

B

Baker, Dean, 36
Baldwin, Chuck, 44
Barr, Bob, 37, 44
Bartlett, Bruce, 37–40
Benjamin, Medea, 26
Bergland, David, 49
Bibby, John F., 8
Biden, Joe, 74
Bipartisan gerrymandering, 69
Black Power advocacy, 29
Bush, George H. W., 26, 62
Bush, George W., 21, 35, 38, 62

C

Cap-and-trade bill, 79
Carter, Jimmy, 56
Centrism of Democratic Party, 24
Chamber of Commerce (U.S.), 56
Charlie Wilson's War movie, 13
Chomsky, Noam, 21
Christian Coalition, 30
Church, Frank, 15
Civil rights legislation (1957), 78

Civil War, 12, 18
Clinton, Bill, 21, 34
Collins, Susan, 13
Committee on Political Parties, 11
Communist Party, 20
Constitutional Convention, 54–55, 78
Constitution Party, 44
Cooke, Shamus, 9
C-SPAN, 38–39

D

Daily Show, 79
Danaher, Kevin, 26
Declaration of Independence, 53
DeLay, Tom, 14, 65, 70
Democratic-Farmer-Labor Party, 76
Democratic National Convention, 32
Democratic Party, 8, 9
    centrism of, 24
    egalitarian identity needs of, 33
    filibuster elimination by, 74
    filibusters by, 77
    Green Party alliance with, 48
    insurgent campaigns, 33–34
    Libertarian Party vs., 39–40
    negative views of, 24–25
    principles of, 14
    progressive groups in, 31
    Republican similarities, 42–43
    Senate majority of, 15
    single-member districts, 20

candidate qualities, 31–34
Electoral College and, 18–20
electoral system trap of, 47–48
encouragement of participation, 18
enjoyability of, 50–51
liberals/citizens hurt by, 23–36
plurality elections and, 21
possibility of success in U.S., 24–27
single-member districts and, 20–21
unwinnability vs. usefulness of, 46–51
Third party voters, 44–45
Thurmond, Strom, 78
"Toward a More Responsible Two-Party System" (Committee on Political Parties), 11
Truman, Harry, 62
Two party electoral system, 18, 42–43
See also Democratic Party; Republican Party

U

U.S. Chamber of Commerce, 56

V

Vermont, 18
Voting vs. winning, 48–50

W

Wallace, George, 42
Wall Street Journal, 7
Washington, George, 78
Welker, Herman, 14–15
Why the Electoral College Is Bad for America (Edwards), 57
Will, George, 61–62
Wilson, Woodrow, 62
Winston, David, 66
"The-worse-the-better" theory, 25–26
Write-in voters, 44–45

Y

Yglesias, Mathew, 11–16